THE ODYSSEY

THE ODYSSEY

screenplay by
CHRISTOPHER NOLAN

Based on
Homer's *Odyssey*

faber

First published in 2026
by Faber & Faber Limited
The Bindery, 51 Hatton Garden
London EC1N 8HN

First published in the USA in 2026

Typeset by Brighton Gray
Printed and bound by CPI Group (UK) Ltd, Croydon CR0 4YY

A CIP record for this book
is available from the British Library

ISBN 978–0–571–40338–7

Printed and bound in the UK on FSC® certified paper in line with our continuing
commitment to ethical business practices, sustainability and the environment.
For further information see faber.co.uk/environmental-policy

Our authorised representative in the EU for product safety is
Easy Access System Europe, Mustamäe tee 50, 10621 Tallinn, Estonia
gpsr.requests@easproject.com

2 4 6 8 10 9 7 5 3 1

Contents

Cast and Credits

MATT DAMON
TOM HOLLAND
ANNE HATHAWAY
ROBERT PATTINSON
LUPITA NYONG'O
SAMANTHA MORTON
JOHN LEGUIZAMO

with

ZENDAYA

and

CHARLIZE THERON

JON BERNTHAL
HIMESH PATEL

BILL IRWIN
ELLIOT PAGE
BENNY SAFDIE

A Universal Pictures
Presentation

A Syncopy
Production

A Film by
CHRISTOPHER NOLAN

THE ODYSSEY

Based on Homer's *Odyssey*

Written for the Screen and Directed by	CHRISTOPHER NOLAN
Produced by	EMMA THOMAS
Produced by	CHRISTOPHER NOLAN
Executive Producer	THOMAS HAYSLIP
Director of Photography	HOYTE VAN HOYTEMA, ASC, FSF, NSC
Production Designer	RUTH DE JONG
Edited by	JENNIFER LAME, ACE
Music by	LUDWIG GÖRANSSON
Visual Effects Supervisor	ANDREW JACKSON
Special Effects Supervisor	SCOTT R. FISHER
Costumes Designed by	ELLEN MIROJNICK
Co-Producers	ANDY THOMPSON HELEN MEDRANO
Casting by	JOHN PAPSIDERA, CSA

THE ODYSSEY

THE SCREENPLAY

BLACK SCREEN.

Silence. Words appear:

'A TIME OF APPARENT MAGIC . . .'

Title slowly FADES as the sound of SURF rises . . .

BANG! A LOUD wooden BEAT –

MALE VOICE
(O.S.)

A face.

BANG!

MALE VOICE
(O.S.)

A fleet.

BANG!

DAY: WAVES CRASH, foam and sand SPRAYS off a FOREIGN SHORE . . .

MALE VOICE
(O.S.)

A war.

. . . some of the foam is RED.

BANG!

NIGHT: a BARD stands atop a long table – TORCHLIGHT hot on UPTURNED FACES – he BEATS the rhythm with his STAFF . . .

MALE VOICE (BARD)

A man.

BANG!

DAY: a FIGURE on the shore, head down in contemplation . . .

BARD
(O.S.)

A thought.

BANG!

NIGHT: the Bard LEANS down to his ENRAPTURED AUDIENCE . . .

BARD

A trick.

BANG!

DAY: a GIANT WOODEN STATUE OF A REARING HORSE, massive, half-buried, listing sickly in wet sand at rising tide . . .

BARD
(O.S.)

A trick to break the walls of Troy.

BANG!

NIGHT: the Bard raises his arms . . .

BARD

And burn it screaming to the ground.

All eyes on his staff as he brings it down –

BANG!

DAY: a wave CRASHES against the Horse, watched by a lone, RAGGED Greek soldier. This is SINON.

At the sound of HOOVES, Sinon TURNS – TROJANS on horseback approach from far down the beach, riding FASTER and FASTER through the DETRITUS of a departed army . . .

THWACK – an ARROW hits his arm – THWACK, THWACK, THWACK – arrow after arrow forces him back until WHUMP – a SPEAR PINS him to the Horse . . .

The Trojans ENCIRCLE, DISMOUNT, APPROACH. They stare up at the giant Horse, indifferent to Sinon's suffering.

FIRST TROJAN

What does it mean?

He DRAWS BRONZE, puts it to Sinon's chin and lifts his head to look into his DYING EYES –

SINON

A gift. For Athena.

The First Trojan swings his sword – a SECOND TROJAN BLOCKS –

SECOND TROJAN

Common Gods. Respect their offering.

He YANKS the spear free, dropping Sinon to the sand.

SECOND TROJAN

(to soldiers)

Save it from the waves. Take it to Athena's temple. The war's over.

A CHEER turns into a CHANT ringing out across the water . . .

HUNDREDS of Trojans throw DOZENS of ROPES around the Horse, DRAGGING it painfully, inch by inch, out of the rising tide . . .

We push in on the Horse as it GRINDS through wet sand, CLOSER and CLOSER on the rough wooden PLANKING, until –

FEMALE VOICE

(O.S.)

STOP!

Cut to:

INT. MEGARON (GREAT HALL), PALACE OF ITHACA – NIGHT

The Bard shoulders his staff. The ROWDY CROWD quiets. All eyes turn to the source of the shout – a FLICKERING SILHOUETTE behind a wooden screen at the top of the stairs, seated at her work. This is PENELOPE. She rises . . .

PENELOPE

Not this song!

A Young Man (twenty) seated off to one side scrambles to his feet. This is TELEMACHUS.

VARIOUS

Uh-oh! Mommy's mad! Run, run!

RAUCOUS LAUGHTER as Telemachus mounts the stairs, sidles up to the screen like a confessional, speaking softly –

TELEMACHUS

I want to remind them whose wine they're drinking.

PENELOPE

I don't want Odysseus's song – I want Odysseus.

TELEMACHUS

Then why do you entertain suitors in his house? Night after night?

PENELOPE

In this world a man does what he chooses. I do what I can.

TELEMACHUS

I'm a man, now, Mom.

PENELOPE

So throw them out. Break Zeus's law, and see what they do to you if you give them that excuse.

Telemachus looks across the raucous crowd of SUITORS feasting –

PENELOPE

I've already lost a husband, I don't want to lose a son.

TELEMACHUS

Dad's coming back.

PENELOPE

Then where is he? *Eight years* since Troy fell. Almost *twenty* since he left us. Where is he?

At the sound of JEERS and SHOUTS, Telemachus TURNS to see a BEGGAR at the door KICKED by one of the Suitors . . . Telemachus HURRIES down the stairs and across the hall –

TELEMACHUS

We have to welcome him like we welcomed all of you!

One of the Suitors bullying the Beggar TURNS on Telemachus. This is POLYBUS (thirties, large, threatening).

POLYBUS

Are you calling us beggars?

TELEMACHUS

I'm saying you've been welcome here . . . For *three years*.

MALE VOICE

(O.S.)

We've only enjoyed your hospitality for so long . . .

Telemachus TURNS. ANTINOUS (thirties, handsome, charismatic), RISES from his place.

ANTINOUS

Because your mother won't choose.

TELEMACHUS

She's already married.

ANTINOUS

Odysseus is dead.

TELEMACHUS

What do you know about my dad?

Antinous tosses back his drink and picks his teeth.

ANTINOUS

I know he kept stringy cattle and bad wine.

TELEMACHUS

You had the best of it the first two seasons.

ANTINOUS

And I know he never came home.

TELEMACHUS

Not yet.

With a glance at Penelope's listening silhouette, Antinous leans in, DISCREET . . .

ANTINOUS

Pining for a daddy you didn't even know like some snivelling bastard.

Telemachus weighs the insult.

TELEMACHUS

None of us can really know who our fathers are. Not even you. So don't claim to know mine.

ANTINOUS

But I did . . .

INSERT CUT: TEENAGE ANTINOUS, amongst other youngsters, crouches in the bushes, clutching an arrow. An OPEN HAND reaches back – all the teenage boys rush to hand it an arrow. The hand takes it from the boy next to Antinous . . .

ANTINOUS

As boys, we watched him hunt. I tried to volunteer for his expedition to Troy, but he told me to stay here and keep an eye on you.

TELEMACHUS

On me or my mother?

Antinous glances at Penelope's silhouette, GRINS.

ANTINOUS

You can't blame me for looking.

TELEMACHUS

My dad's coming home. And his hospitality won't be as generous as hers.

ANTINOUS

(amused)

He doesn't follow Zeus's law?

TELEMACHUS

Zeus's law tells us to treat strangers as we'd be treated because they might be Gods in disguise. I think we've established you're not a God, Antinous.

Polybus lifts the Beggar's ragged robe . . .

POLYBUS

He doesn't smell like a God.

TELEMACHUS

It wouldn't be much of a disguise if he did . . .

Telemachus takes the Beggar by the arm.

TELEMACHUS

Careful, he might strike you down right now.

THUNDER echoes through the halls . . . Polybus stands down. The crowd QUIETS. Telemachus leads the beggar to his own table, off to the side.

BEGGAR

That thunder was luck.

Telemachus peers into the grey eyes of the stranger . . .

TELEMACHUS

I don't know, you have wise eyes. Athena's eyes.

The Beggar smiles. Shakes his head.

TELEMACHUS

Sit. Eat.

BEGGAR

Thank you.

The Beggar starts to eat, hungrily.

TELEMACHUS

You sailed with traders?

BEGGAR

From Sparta.

TELEMACHUS

Has Menelaus come home from the war?

BEGGAR

Years ago. Odysseus never came back?

TELEMACHUS

We don't even know if he's alive. Have you heard anything?

BEGGAR

The song of how he won the war.

TELEMACHUS

We've all heard that. Nothing else?

BEGGAR

No, but Sparta's full of Trojan War veterans – someone'll know something.

The Beggar studies Telemachus with kind eyes.

BEGGAR

You're Odysseus's son? Go to Sparta. Go see Menelaus – he'd welcome you.

Telemachus considers this. A maid, MELANTHO, approaches.

MELANTHO

The Queen wants to speak to the stranger.

The Beggar, surprised, looks at Telemachus.

TELEMACHUS

She lives for news.

The Beggar nods, rises. Telemachus grabs his hand.

TELEMACHUS

Just don't try to give her false hope. She has some way of knowing whether a person has actually seen Odysseus. See that man?

The Beggar looks at a rough older man sitting at the side, listening without seeing. This is EUMAEUS.

TELEMACHUS

My dad's most loyal worker. He can't see much any more . . .

By feel, Eumaeus offers a chop to an elderly dog, ARGUS.

TELEMACHUS

But that doesn't stop him beating travellers to death in exchange for lies about my father.

The Beggar, nervous, is led to sit on the stairs in front of the screen by Penelope's silhouette at her loom.

EXT. CLIFFS OF ITHACA – DAY

Bronze CLASHES BRIGHTLY as Telemachus TRAINS with an older man, MENTOR (forties). Eumaeus supervises, elderly Argus limp at his feet.

EUMAEUS

Too fast.

Telemachus turns, breathless. Mentor lowers his sword.

TELEMACHUS

How can you know?

EUMAEUS

You don't need eyes to hear a hasty combination. Mentor, push him.

Mentor LASHES out – Telemachus MEETS each blow –

EUMAEUS

Too fast.

Telemachus stops, frustrated, slumps down next to Eumaeus. He reaches out to pet Argus who GROWLS . . .

TELEMACHUS

He's as friendly as you.

EUMAEUS

He only answered to your father.

Telemachus gently rubs the dog's thinning fur.

TELEMACHUS

Where did he get him from?

EUMAEUS

They met right here . . .

EXT. SAME – DAY (FLASHBACK)

Eumaeus (younger, sighted) sorts a litter of PUPPIES *by* TOSSING *the runts off the cliff. He lifts one up to look at its half-closed eyes. Frowns, starts to* TOSS *when his arm is* GRABBED *– Eumaeus turns to –*

ODYSSEUS *(thirties, short dark beard, handsome, rugged), looking at the runt, a smile playing about his lips . . .*

ODYSSEUS

I'll take him.

EUMAEUS

For your boy?

ODYSSEUS

For a hunting dog.

Eumaeus SNORTS.

EXT. SAME – DAY (PRESENT)

Eumaeus feels for Argus's stiff, mangey fur.

EUMAEUS

Damned if he wasn't right.

Telemachus watches Eumaeus remember . . .

EXT. WILDS OF ITHACA – DAY (FLASHBACK)

Argus (young but fully grown) has eyes fixed on a WILD BOAR *feeding yards away. At his side,* ODYSSEUS *carefully* STRINGS *his massive hunting bow. Behind him several* TEENAGE BOYS *watch him, wide-eyed. Odysseus reaches back for an arrow – all the teenage boys rush to hand him one. He takes it from the* SMALLEST, *the* TEENAGE SINON.

Eumaeus watches as Odysseus PLUCKS *the string with a* MIGHTY TWANG *– the Boar* LOOKS *up –* CHARGES . . .

Odysseus fixes arrow to bow, horizontal, aiming – TEENAGE ANTINOUS BOLTS, TERRIFIED *– the other boys, except Sinon,* FOLLOW *– Odysseus* FIRES *– hits the Boar in the chest – it* KEEPS COMING, COMING . . . GORES *his leg . . . Argus throws himself at the Boar's neck with* LOYAL SAVAGERY . . .

EXT. COURTYARD, PALACE OF ITHACA – DAY (FLASHBACK)

Eumaeus watches an OLD NURSEMAID *stitch the wound in Odysseus's leg.*

EUMAEUS

Why do you always pluck your bow?

ODYSSEUS

To test the tension.

Eumaeus looks at him. Not buying it.

ODYSSEUS

Ouch!

The Old Nursemaid looks at him, annoyed.

OLD NURSEMAID

Hold still. How bad a scar do you want?

ODYSSEUS

(*to Eumaeus*)

It's only fair.

EUMAEUS

To warn your prey?

ODYSSEUS

To fight with honour.

EUMAEUS

You weren't fighting – you were hunting.

ODYSSEUS

Hunting's just fighting by stealth.

EUMAEUS

Clever. But your cleverness will get you in trouble.

EXT. CLIFFS OF ITHACA – DAY (PRESENT)

Eumaeus puts his hand on Telemachus's shoulder.

EUMAEUS

Try again. This time not as fast. Or precise.

Telemachus gets to his feet. Mentor raises his guard. Eumaeus pulls Telemachus down to WHISPER in his ear.

EUMAEUS

(whisper)

You can't win with a perfect defence. Draw the attack.

TELEMACHUS

How?

EUMAEUS

(whisper)

Hesitation. Open your belly to your opponent's blade – their attack becomes *your* chance . . .

Telemachus straightens up. He and Mentor SPAR . . . Telemachus opens his defence – Mentor overextends – Telemachus moves outside the thrust – finishes with his sword at Mentor's throat. He nods, satisfied.

TELEMACHUS

Did you teach my father that?

EUMAEUS

No, he taught me. He said you're not always going to be the strongest or the fastest. So be the smartest.

TELEMACHUS

What would he do if he came back here to find these suitors in his house?

Eumaeus shakes his head with LONGING . . .

EUMAEUS

Don't. I can't even let myself imagine what he'd do to them.

TELEMACHUS

There's so many.

EUMAEUS

Cut a couple down, the others cave. Bullies and cowards. Most of them were old enough to go to Troy. But when they saw Agamemnon's sail . . .

EXT. SAME – DAY (FLASHBACK)

Odysseus and Eumaeus watch SHIPS *approach. The lead ship has a* BLACK SAIL . . .

EUMAEUS

(V.O.)

Their fathers hid them. Odysseus didn't judge. You and your mother meant more to him than promises of glory . . .

Odysseus looks at Eumaeus. Concerned.

INSERT CUT: ODYSSEUS AND PENELOPE PLAY WITH THE INFANT TELEMACHUS . . .

An imposing figure in extraordinary BLACKENED BRONZE ARMOUR *approaches Odysseus. This is* AGAMEMNON. *Odysseus* KNEELS *before him. Agamemnon pulls Odysseus to his feet in brotherly embrace . . .*

EUMAEUS
(V.O.)
And he knew Agamemnon's war would take many lives and many years.

Odysseus, TEARS *down his cheeks, looks at Agamemnon. Nods.*

EUMAEUS
(V.O.)
So he raised his army by lottery.

INSERT CUT: *a* LINE *of* YOUNG MEN *snakes up the hillside to where Eumaeus is taking their lots . . . Teenage Sinon and Teenage Antinous reach the front of the line together . . .*

TELEMACHUS
By lots? Antinous told me he volunteered . . .

Eumaeus shifts, uncomfortable.

EUMAEUS
That's how your father talked about it.

INSERT CUT: *Eumaeus waves Odysseus over to talk to Teenage Sinon and Teenage Antinous. Teenage Antinous is holding a* WOODEN LOT *with* NOTCHES *in its side . . . Odysseus listens to their pleas. He takes the lot from Teenage Antinous and hands it to Teenage Sinon.* HE WAVES ANTINOUS'S FATHER *over . . .*

ODYSSEUS
Your boy tried to take Sinon's place. I'm not letting him. He needs to stay here and look after his family.

ANTINOUS'S FATHER *looks at Odysseus, tearfully grateful . . .*

ANTINOUS'S FATHER

He can watch over your boy, too.

ODYSSEUS

Of course.

EXT. CLIFFS OF ITHACA – DAY (PRESENT)

Telemachus looks at Eumaeus, incredulous.

TELEMACHUS

He wanted Antinous to look after me?

Eumaeus SPITS into the dust.

EUMAEUS

No. But Odysseus was sensitive to a father's shame. He felt for these fathers . . . he knew it was an unwinnable war . . .

Telemachus listens to the story.

EUMAEUS

Then, somehow, he won it.

Telemachus nods with pride.

TELEMACHUS

So he *knew* it would be years. Did he tell my mother?

Eumaeus shifts, uncomfortable . . .

EUMAEUS

That's a question for her.

He gets to his feet.

TELEMACHUS

Eumaeus? Is he ever coming back?

Eumaeus frowns.

EUMAEUS

Argus thinks so. I've never known a dog reach twenty . . .

Eumaeus wipes a quiet tear . . .

EUMAEUS

But he's long outlived his master.

INT. MEGARON, PALACE OF ITHACA – DAY

Telemachus mounts the stairs, approaches the screen and SLIDES it back to reveal . . .

INT. THE QUEEN'S CHAMBER – DAY

Penelope at her loom. She is BEAUTIFUL, ELEGANT (forties). She pauses in her weaving. Melantho and the Old Nursemaid are seated nearby.

TELEMACHUS

I didn't mean to stop you.

Penelope nods at Melantho who checks there is no one beyond the screen as she draws it closed behind Telemachus. She gives Penelope the okay.

PENELOPE

I'm in no hurry. The Elders decreed that when I finish your grandfather's burial shroud it'll be time to remarry.

Penelope rises from her loom.

TELEMACHUS

Why?

She leads him out onto the terrace.

EXT. PENELOPE'S TERRACE, PALACE OF ITHACA – CONTINUOUS

They walk out onto the terrace.

PENELOPE

Ithaca's been without a king for too long. They want security.

TELEMACHUS

From what?

PENELOPE

The people from the sea.

Telemachus SCOFFS at this.

TELEMACHUS

Travellers' tales.

PENELOPE

All we know of the world is travellers' tales! That's how we heard Troy had fallen. Now they all tell stories of attacks by people from the sea.

TELEMACHUS

Who are?

PENELOPE

Nobody knows. But the Elders want Ithaca to be prepared.

TELEMACHUS

Prepared? We're part of the greatest civilization ever known.

PENELOPE

Look at this great house –

Penelope places a gentle hand on the stone of the battlements.

PENELOPE

Stones as old as knowledge. At the mercy of some greedy unwanted guests. Half the servants answer to *them* now. The structure's nothing without people's respect for its meaning.

TELEMACHUS

Zeus's law.

PENELOPE

Treat others as you'd be treated. When they abuse it, they destroy everything.

TELEMACHUS

So how could you think of marrying one of them?

Penelope considers how to answer.

PENELOPE

Because, a long time ago, your father asked me to . . .

INT. BEDCHAMBER – NIGHT (FLASHBACK)

Penelope and Odysseus lie on the bed. The INFANT *Telemachus plays on cushions and furs laid out on the floor.*

ODYSSEUS

Agamemnon is our king. The Trojans took his brother's wife.

PENELOPE

Or she ran away with them.

ODYSSEUS

Either way, the Trojans will never give Helen up. And the walls of Troy are said to be impregnable. We'll sit outside that great city trying to draw them into battle. As years go by, and Telemachus grows, and you learn life without me.

PENELOPE

Don't. I'll raise our boy and manage our kingdom until you return. Menelaus will give up on Helen.

Odysseus shakes his head, resigned.

ODYSSEUS

This is Agamemnon's excuse to break Troy's control of the trading routes. He won't let it pass. Ever.

PENELOPE

What if you refuse?

Odysseus looks at the infant Telemachus, now FAST ASLEEP, *then back to Penelope. He does not want to answer.*

ODYSSEUS

He'll take our son.

PENELOPE

He would never – !

ODYSSEUS

He sacrificed his own daughter for favourable winds.

INSERT CUT: WE FOLLOW AGAMEMNON, IN HIS ARMOUR, CARRYING AN ADOLESCENT GIRL TOWARDS A STORMY SEA . . .

Penelope takes this in. Appalled.

PENELOPE

Why would the Gods want his daughter's life?

ODYSSEUS

The power of a sacrifice is in the cost to the person making it.

PENELOPE

That's monstrous.

ODYSSEUS

And committed. I won't return soon. If at all.

Penelope considers this. Suddenly –

PENELOPE

What if we ran?

She lifts up on the bed, excited . . .

PENELOPE

Took your fastest ship and brightest crew and headed for the horizon?

INSERT CUT: Penelope, BABY TELEMACHUS in her arms, and Odysseus stand on the prow of a ship, rowing westward at dusk . . .

PENELOPE
(V.O.)

Held hands on deck as we sailed into the unknown west . . .

Penelope's eyes glitter with excitement . . .

PENELOPE

Chasing the escaping sun . . .

Penelope looks into Odysseus's eyes. Sees his longing . . .

PENELOPE

There's a world beyond these walls.

Odysseus shakes off her vision.

ODYSSEUS

Agamemnon's vengeance would fall on all of Ithaca.

Odysseus looks at Penelope.

ODYSSEUS

Promise me. If I'm not back by the time Telemachus comes of age – promise you'll take another husband –

Penelope SMACKS *his face.*

ODYSSEUS

Enough sacrifices. Promise me.

PENELOPE

Love isn't a sacrifice.

ODYSSEUS

Of course it is. And I don't want you to make it.

PENELOPE

That's not up to you.

ODYSSEUS

Promise me.

She looks into his eyes. Sees love asking.

PENELOPE

No. Promise me you'll come back.

Odysseus looks at this woman. Wanting to be everything for her.

ODYSSEUS

What if I can't?

PENELOPE

Then your memory won't be making my decisions.

She lies back, showing him a decorative pin of Athena on her breast.

PENELOPE

Take my pin. Wear it. Always. Athena will bring you back.

Odysseus looks at the pin, smiling.

ODYSSEUS

I'm not sure it suits me.

PENELOPE

When travellers claim to have seen you, I'll ask them what you were wearing . . .

Odysseus removes the pin from her dress, opening it . . .

PENELOPE

And I'll know if they're lying.

Odysseus and Penelope embrace, losing themselves in each other.

EXT. PENELOPE'S TERRACE, PALACE OF ITHACA – DAY (PRESENT)

Penelope heads back inside . . .

PENELOPE

If the Sea People are real . . . right now Ithaca has no king to raise an army.

INT. PENELOPE'S CHAMBER, PALACE OF ITHACA – CONTINUOUS

Telemachus follows Penelope back to her loom . . .

TELEMACHUS

I could take the throne.

Penelope looks at her son with the faintest edge of scorn.

She goes to the wall, where Odysseus's HUNTING BOW is displayed, its string wound around it. She pulls it down, THRUSTS it at Telemachus.

PENELOPE

String it.

Telemachus takes it.

TELEMACHUS

That's not –

PENELOPE

String it.

Telemachus unwinds the string, puts one end of the bow to the floor and tries to bend the bow to hook the string on the top. With ALL HIS STRENGTH, he cannot bend the bow enough. Penelope takes the bow back . . .

TELEMACHUS

That's not fair. You said only he could string that bow.

PENELOPE

He was happy to let others try . . .

INT. MEGARON, PALACE OF ITHACA – NIGHT (FLASHBACK)

Servants move the table, lever up the flagstones, drive the axes into the dirt in a line of SIX 'X' SHAPES . . .

PENELOPE

(V.O.)

He'd line up the axes . . .

Odysseus laughs as one of his men fails to string the bow. He takes it and calmly bends the bow to string it. Sits at the end of the hall. He PLUCKS *the bow, sounding a resonant note, raises the bow horizontally, fixes an* ARROW, DRAWS *and* FIRES . . .

As the arrow flies through the crosses of axes and STICKS *into an upturned table, the hall erupts in a* CHEER –

INT. PENELOPE'S CHAMBER, PALACE OF ITHACA – DAY (PRESENT)

Penelope looks down on the bow with great pride . . .

PENELOPE

No one else ever did it.

TELEMACHUS

Mom, they're bleeding us dry so you'll be forced to choose one of them before I can claim the throne myself. The traveller told me Menelaus returned years ago. They've all returned –

PENELOPE

All who survived. Maybe he *is* dead.

TELEMACHUS

And if he is, this is my palace. We need to know. I need to go to Menelaus and find out the truth.

Penelope looks at him, surprised.

PENELOPE

Telemachus, these suitors mean you harm.

TELEMACHUS

You think I don't know that? Every night they push me to give them the excuse they need.

PENELOPE

Out there on the sea, on the road . . . they won't need an excuse – you just won't come back.

Telemachus looks at her. Suspicious.

TELEMACHUS

You don't want me to claim the throne myself. You want to keep me in my place. So you can stay Queen of Ithaca.

PENELOPE

(frustrated)

I've had enough of being Queen of Ithaca without my King.

TELEMACHUS

Without *your* king . . . or without *a* king?

Penelope shakes her head, frustrated.

PENELOPE

And you think you're ready to take your father's place. You're a child.

She goes back to her work.

INT. MEGARON, PALACE OF ITHACA – NIGHT

Telemachus, fuming, watches the Suitors FEAST.

Eumaeus, sitting at the side, hears a male servant come rushing, SPURS JANGLING – he STICKS out a restraining hand – his palm hitting the middle of the servant's chest.

EUMAEUS

Too loud, Melanthius. Don't wear your spurs in the palace. You're a cowherd not a horseman.

The Servant, MELANTHIUS, turns on Eumaeus.

MELANTHIUS

And you're a pig farmer. Who're you to talk to me like that?

EUMAEUS

The servant our master left in charge of his herdsmen.

MELANTHIUS

That master's long gone, you blind old fool. You're as welcome here as that old dog bothering the suitors . . .

EUMAEUS

Argus?

Eumaeus shuffles over to the table, trying to find Argus.

EUMAEUS

Argus?

Polybus notices the old dog at his feet. He KICKS it away in disgust – Argus WHIMPERS.

EUMAEUS

Hey! He didn't do anything.

POLYBUS

So that stink is you?

Laughter. Telemachus, blood up, comes over. Antinous watches, interested.

TELEMACHUS

Leave the old dog alone.

POLYBUS

Which one?

EUMAEUS

Both of us.

POLYBUS

What did you say to me, slave?

TELEMACHUS

He got carried away. Argus is my father's hunting dog.

Polybus LAUGHS.

POLYBUS

Hunting dog? Look at that thing. Get it out of here, we're trying to eat –

Polybus KICKS Argus again.

TELEMACHUS

Don't! Can't you hear it's in pain?

POLYBUS

Okay . . .

Polybus GRABS Argus . . .

POLYBUS

I'll put it out of its misery.

EUMAEUS

Leave him alone!

Eumaeus GRABS Polybus's arm – Polybus KICKS him away –

Telemachus, enraged, rushes to the wall, pulling a SWORD from its place and rushing towards Polybus – SWINGING –

Polybus DROPS the dog, DODGES the reckless attack, SMASHING Telemachus to the floor, disarming him and raising the sword –

ANTINOUS

Easy, Polybus.

Antinous steps up beside Polybus . . .

POLYBUS

You saw! You all saw! He attacked me! I have the right!

PENELOPE

(O.S.)

Please!

Penelope slides back the screen, SHOWING HERSELF to the Suitors. The hall falls quiet.

PENELOPE

Please don't hurt my son . . .

Antinous looks at Penelope, then turns back to Polybus –

ANTINOUS

The young pup lost his head. Show some mercy . . .

Antinous gently takes the sword from Polybus . . .

ANTINOUS

Drink some more of his wine, I'll take care of this.

Antinous scoops up the limp Argus. Telemachus gets up –

TELEMACHUS

That's my father's dog! He's only living to see Odysseus return.

ANTINOUS

Fine. I'll put him on the dung heap out front so he can greet his master a little sooner.

As cruel LAUGHTER erupts, Antinous steps across the threshold and DROPS him onto the dung pile in the courtyard. He comes back in, maintaining eye contact with Telemachus. Eumaeus places a restraining hand on Telemachus's arm. Antinous comes close . . .

ANTINOUS

The dog stays out there.

(indicates Eumaeus)

Maybe think twice before you offer up your life for an animal.

Telemachus GLARES at Antinous . . . then TURNS and leaves –

INT. CORRIDOR, PALACE OF ITHACA – MOMENTS LATER

Telemachus stalks down the corridor. He grabs the Old Nursemaid.

TELEMACHUS

Prepare supplies, get them down to the ships. Tell no one. Use only the people you trust.

OLD NURSEMAID

You'll break your mother's heart.

TELEMACHUS

If I stay, they'll force me to fight. No one will back me. I have to find out what happened to my father. Ithaca will be behind me if they know Odysseus is dead.

OLD NURSEMAID

The suitors aren't going to let that happen. You'll never make it back alive.

TELEMACHUS

Tell Mentor to meet me at the ships just before dawn.

OLD NURSEMAID

What should I tell your mother?

TELEMACHUS

Nothing, till we're out of sight of land. Then tell her to hold out as long as she can.

EXT. DOCKS, ITHACA – FIRST LIGHT

Telemachus makes his way to a ship. Mentor falls in beside him.

MENTOR

Ship's ready. Tide's right.

They step onto the ship.

EXT. SHIP – MOMENTS LATER

As the ship casts off. Telemachus and Mentor look out to the brightening horizon.

TELEMACHUS

You haven't even asked where we're going.

Mentor smiles.

TELEMACHUS

I never noticed before. You have wise eyes. Athena's eyes.

MENTOR

Where *are* we going?

TELEMACHUS

To find my dad. He's alive. I feel it in the wind, in the waves . . . he's out there somewhere. Wandering. Injured. Imprisoned, I don't know . . . but alive . . .

And we CUT TO:

EXT. ROCKY BEACH – DAY

We approach a figure staring out at the ocean. ODYSSEUS, now fifty, grizzled, HEAVY GREY BEARD and eyes that have seen too much, trying to solve an impossible riddle –

INSERT CUT: in CLAUSTROPHOBIC DARKNESS packed with MEN, Odysseus pulls himself up out of RISING WATER. A warrior below him is submerged – Odysseus hands him a REED to breathe through . . .

Odysseus PUZZLES over the image, walks through the shallows to where a piece of WEATHERED WOOD protrudes . . .

FEMALE VOICE

(O.S.)

More dreams?

A dark-haired WOMAN in her twenties with GREY EYES is next to him. THIS IS ATHENA.

ODYSSEUS

(puzzled)

Men drowning. Inside . . . some . . . dark space . . .

INSERT CUT: a STONE HEAD from a STATUE of Athena settles on dirty marble, ROCKING from side to side in FLICKERING FIRELIGHT . . .

ODYSSEUS

Firelight on stone . . . I don't know.

He shakes off the image, pulls the plank from the water, brushing his rough hands across the bleached smooth surface of the plank . . .

ATHENA

Don't you want to remember?

He turns to her, frustrated –

ODYSSEUS

Why can't Gods speak in ways we understand?

She shakes her head at him.

ATHENA

Who doesn't understand thunder? Or fire? A child's smile? Or a good harvest?

ODYSSEUS

But you hide yourselves from us.

She points at the sky . . .

ATHENA

Just look – who's moving that cloud or massing those birds? Or darkening the sky?

Odysseus looks at the sky. When he turns back, Athena is GONE . . .

From farther out in the shallows, a BEAUTIFUL BLONDE WOMAN approaches carrying a short spear and fish . . . This is CALYPSO.

CALYPSO

Who were you talking to?

She drops her spear and fish and crouches next to him.

Odysseus looks down at the wood in his hands, tosses it further up onto the sand, where there are other, similar planks . . .

ODYSSEUS

Athena came to me again.

Odysseus looks at the setting sun . . .

INSERT CUT: a STATUE of Athena is STRUCK with a BRONZE SWORD, SPARKING, BEHEADING, TUMBLING amid FIRELIGHT on STONE . . .

ODYSSEUS

She's telling me to remember . . .

He turns to Calypso.

ODYSSEUS

To leave.

CALYPSO

Why would you leave? We have everything we need.

ODYSSEUS

How long have I been here?

Calypso says nothing. Odysseus turns to her.

ODYSSEUS

I have a home somewhere . . . there's someone . . . out there . . .

CALYPSO

How do you know?

ODYSSEUS

I don't know. I *feel*.

Calypso puts her hand on his face. Intimate. Sympathetic. Dry thunder rumbles – she glances up at the sky . . .

INT. CALYPSO'S CAVE – NIGHT

Odysseus and Calypso sit eating the fish she caught.

CALYPSO

What we have here can last forever.

ODYSSEUS

Forever is for Gods. Are you a God?

CALYPSO

Would you stay if I were?

ODYSSEUS

No.

Calypso takes his hands in hers.

CALYPSO

You want to remember. But what if remembering destroys your happiness?

ODYSSEUS

Then it wasn't real. Or earned.

Calypso stares back at him. A peal of dry THUNDER. Letting go of his hands, she glances at the sky. Odysseus reaches for more food, pulling a bowl of MEATY LEAVES towards him –

CALYPSO

No more.

ODYSSEUS

But I love it.

She pulls his plate away from him.

CALYPSO

Stop eating the lotus, and tell me what you remember. After Troy.

Odysseus sparks to the word –

ODYSSEUS

Troy. Years at Troy.

INSERT CUT: in CLAUSTROPHOBIC darkness, the WATER keeps RISING – the man next to Odysseus starts to PANIC – Odysseus covers the man's mouth, holding him dangerously TIGHT . . .

ODYSSEUS

We won the war . . .

CALYPSO

And then?

As Odysseus concentrates, remembering, we CUT TO:

EXT. BEACH AT TROY – DAY

Odysseus (forties, weary but younger, darker, shorter beard) stands in the DUNES looking down at ONE FRESH GRAVE amidst ROWS and ROWS of them. He looks at something in his hand – a WOODEN LOT with NOTCHES on its side. He puts the lot deep in his belt.

Odysseus follows Agamemnon to his ship. Behind them, above the dunes, smoke rises over the smouldering ruins of the greatest city ever known. Odysseus kisses Agamemnon.

Agamemnon's ships pull away. Odysseus approaches his men, scattered amongst the dunes.

ODYSSEUS

Ten years on this fucking beach.

He looks around for better words. There aren't any.

ODYSSEUS

Let's go home. Remember those we leave here.

His men, three ships' worth, hardened, exhausted, filthy, nod reverently. Several in tears. A Soldier, EURYLOCHUS, comes close . . .

EURYLOCHUS

Do we have enough provisions?

ODYSSEUS

We've taken enough from Troy. An extra stop or two won't slow us down.

EXT. ODYSSEUS'S SHIP – DAY

Odysseus watches the Helmsman, ANTIPHATES. Checks the sail.

ODYSSEUS

Stow the oars.

A cheer from the men. Odysseus smiles to himself. Looks left and right to his other two ships.

ODYSSEUS

Follow the southerly winds.

ANTIPHATES

Yes, sir.

EURYLOCHUS

Agamemnon's rowing west, along the known provisions route.

ODYSSEUS

He's got more mouths to feed. We'll find places to land.

EURYLOCHUS

Are you sure? It's a risk.

ODYSSEUS

I've followed Agamemnon long enough.

As the Helmsman brings the ship around, Odysseus looks at the tiny dots of Agamemnon's sails heading west.

ODYSSEUS

With a little luck and the right winds, we'll see some of the world, and still be home before Agamemnon.

ODYSSEUS

(O.S.)

We set off for home . . .

EXT. ODYSSEUS'S SHIP – DAY

Odysseus and Eurylochus watch a lush shore come into view.

ODYSSEUS

See?

EURYLOCHUS

Lucky bastard. We're down to our last supplies.

Odysseus turns to another one of his men, POLITES –

ODYSSEUS

Assemble a landing party. Food and water. Enough for three weeks.

POLITES

What if they won't give it?

EURYLOCHUS

How badly do you want to go home?

ODYSSEUS

(*V.O.*)

Begging, trading or plundering . . .

EXT. COASTAL VILLAGE – TWILIGHT

Eurylochus interrogates a kneeling OLD MAN. Men carry SACKS and JARS down to the sea. A soldier, ELPENOR, translates.

ODYSSEUS

(*V.O.*)

Depending on our needs.

EURYLOCHUS

Ask him why they abandoned their village instead of welcoming us.

ELPENOR

He says they thought we were the Sea People.

Eurylochus crouches to look the old man in the eye.

EURYLOCHUS

No, we're Greeks. From Ithaca. Maybe you heard of our victory at Troy?

(*Nothing.*)

We're heading west on the southerly winds.

Nothing. Eurylochus rises. The Old Man starts talking.

ELPENOR

He says if we go that way . . . we won't like the things we'll find.

Eurylochus nods at Polites who puts a torch to a thatched roof . . .

ODYSSEUS
(V.O.)

After years of war . . .

Eurylochus heads back to shore amongst his plundering men . . .

ODYSSEUS
(V.O)

. . . no one could stand between my men and home.

INT. CALYPSO'S CAVE – NIGHT

ODYSSEUS

Not even me . . .

CALYPSO

But something happened?

Odysseus puzzles it out, his mind unclouding . . .

EXT. ODYSSEUS'S SHIP – DAY

Odysseus is slumped on the deck, tying knots.

SAILOR

Land!

Odysseus jumps to his feet with the other men, crowding the rail. In the distance, an ISLAND. Odysseus turns to Eurylochus, grinning.

ODYSSEUS

There you go.

EURYLOCHUS

Lucky bastard.

EXT. BAY OF ISLAND – DAY

The three ships glide into the bay of the lush island.

ODYSSEUS

Signal the others to anchor here for tonight. We'll head in.

EXT. ISLAND SHORE – EVENING

The lone ship beaches. Odysseus and his men get off and look cautiously at the thick forest.

EURYLOCHUS

It's late. We should camp till dawn.

ODYSSEUS

There's time. Leave a watch. Come on . . .

Odysseus heads into the forest, excited. His men follow. Some are uneasy, but all are happy to touch dry land.

EXT. FOREST – LATER

Odysseus spots a SHEEP. Eurylochus raises his bow, but Odysseus puts a restraining hand on his arm.

ODYSSEUS

Sheep come in flocks. Let's follow.

They quietly follow the sheep in the darkening forest . . .

They emerge into a clearing overlooked by a LARGE CAVE MOUTH . . .

The sheep wanders into the dark of the cave. Odysseus follows . . .

INT. CAVE, ISLAND – CONTINUOUS

Odysseus and his men make their way into the VAST CAVE . . . a MASSIVE ROCK by the entrance . . . darker and darker . . .

a smouldering fire. Stacks of large CHEESES . . . the sheep, lying deep in the cave, watches, disinterested . . .

EURYLOCHUS

Someone lives here.

Odysseus samples one of the cheeses.

ODYSSEUS

They make pretty good cheese.

EURYLOCHUS

We should leave. We've brought nothing to trade with.

ODYSSEUS

Zeus's law.

Eurylochus looks around the cave, trying to fathom who might live such a place . . .

EURYLOCHUS

I don't know if whoever lives here's heard of Zeus's law. Or Zeus, for that matter.

ODYSSEUS

Everyone knows Zeus's law. Get the fire going. We'll welcome the owner back.

Odysseus is examining several tree trunks lying around, CARVED into tapering shapes.

A SUDDEN RUSH OF HOOFBEATS, they all turn to the bright end of the cave, a hundred yards away, as a FLOCK of SHEEP, RAMS, and GOATS comes running in from the light . . .

The animals surround the men, bleating. A DULL THUDDING shakes the earth . . . all eyes turn to the bright mouth of the cave as . . .

A MONSTROUS SILHOUETTE lowers its head to enter. Odysseus and his men stand, frozen, as the GIANT SHAPE DRAGS the massive rock across the cave entrance . . .

TOTAL DARKNESS. The gentle movement and bleating of the settling flock . . . WHISPERS amongst Odysseus's men . . .

EURYLOCHUS
(whisper)

What is that?

ODYSSEUS

Shhh . . .

The men instinctively GATHER around the BRIGHTENING FIRE . . .

NOISES OF SCALE – movement, scratching, OCEAN-DEEP BREATHS . . . Odysseus sees his men gathered at the fire – gestures –

ODYSSEUS
(low)

Get away from the fire.

His men look at him, uncomprehending. A Soldier on the far side looks at Odysseus, terrified –

WHOOOOSH – a fleeting impression of a GIANT HAND and he's YANKED, SCREAMING, into darkness . . .

The Soldiers SCAMPER into the darkness . . .

The SCREAM is CUT OFF. The sound of QUIET, MASSIVE CHEWING . . .

CLANG! BLOODY ARMOUR hits the ground near the fire.

ODYSSEUS

Spread out!

Odysseus moves away from where he shouted, FEELS the WHOOSH of a giant hand blowing past him in the dark . . . he stops, crouched low, ready to run, peering into the dark . . . by the fire, a massive FOOT and KNEE COME down, dimly lit . . . suddenly a COLOSSAL FACE moves into the light, low above the fire, PEERING with a SINGLE GIANT EYE into the flames . . . a CYCLOPS.

The Cyclops reaches into the fire and pulls out a flaming log. RISES, holding the log like a large match, PEERING around with its GROTESQUE WATERY EYE, rolling in its socket, LIP-LIKE LIDS slow blinking moisture onto its glassy membrane . . . peering into darkness . . . until . . .

A Soldier SCREAMS as he is grabbed and shoved SQUIRMING into the Cyclops's mouth . . . the Cyclops DROPS the burning log to use both hands to remove the indigestible sword and armour of the soldier like a child eating a shrimp . . .

CYCLOPS

MMMMMMMMMMM . . .

Odysseus, in the dark, makes out a Soldier near him, shivering. Odysseus nods, trying to reassure.

By the fire, the Cyclops lowers itself to the ground, lying near the fire and closing its eye, blood dribbling from the corner of its mouth.

INT. SAME – LATER

Odysseus nudges the soldier.

ODYSSEUS

(whispers)

I think it's asleep.

Odysseus makes his way over to the SLEEPING MAMMOTH. The other Soldiers emerge to assemble by the monstrous head. Eurylochus draws his sword, and considers how to kill the Cyclops. His men MIME different killing zones, bringing fingers across necks, wrists, behind the ear . . .

Eurylochus chooses a spot, lines up his sword, when Odysseus stops him, pointing into the dark away from the fire. Eurylochus does not understand . . .

ODYSSEUS
(whispers)

The rock.

Eurylochus gets it, moves away from the Cyclops to talk.

EURYLOCHUS

We can't move the rock.

ODYSSEUS

We'd be trapped in here.

Odysseus thinks.

ODYSSEUS

Spread the word. Rest up. In the morning, when it lets out its flock we'll rush the entrance. It can't grab all of us.

Eurylochus nods. They settle down for the night.

Odysseus watches as the fire dies . . .

INT. SAME – MORNING

Odysseus is woken by a GRINDING NOISE as LIGHT floods into the cave. The silhouette of the Cyclops has rolled back the giant boulder. The sheep BLEAT as they start gathering near the entrance . . . Odysseus looks around at his men, all around the cave, preparing to rush the door . . .

The Cyclops steps into the cave towards them to pick up its tree trunk club . . .

Odysseus starts to run . . . his men do the same, racing towards the DAZZLING light of the cave entrance –

BOOM! A GIANT FOOT comes down as the Cyclops steps over them once . . . BOOM! The other foot comes down on a Soldier, crushing him . . . as fast as they sprint, the Cyclops is already back in front of them, crouching, feeling the tops of the sheep as they pass by . . . it GRABS the Soldier next to Odysseus, giving Odysseus a chance to race beneath it . . . he is in the light now, home free, but he turns and sees the Cyclops tossing and pushing half his men back into the dark . . . Eurylochus is beside him . . . the Cyclops grabs the boulder, starting to close up the cave . . .

ODYSSEUS

It's shutting them in! Go! Get them down to the ships!

Odysseus races back, past the Cyclops's foot, into the dark just as the Cyclops SHUTS them in.

INT. CAVE, ISLAND – LATER

Odysseus and his men are gathered by the fire.

POLITES

Could we jam something in the cave mouth to leave a gap?

ODYSSEUS

Maybe. But what?

Elpenor speaks up –

ELPENOR

This log?

Odysseus looks at the large log.

ODYSSEUS

It'll notice.

Odysseus gets up and looks closer as the log. It tapers.

ODYSSEUS

Grab the thin end. Put it in the fire.

His men start to work.

ODYSSEUS

How much rope do we have?

Soldiers start unwinding rope from their waists . . . Odysseus counts his men . . .

ODYSSEUS

How big's the flock?

ANTIPHATES

Two dozen, maybe?

ODYSSEUS

Not enough for all of us. When he comes back, two of us have to get out.

LAODAMAS

Or at least get killed.

Two soldiers step forward, CEPHEUS and one other.

ODYSSEUS

Run low through the flock towards the entrance, then split wide –

POLITES

So he can only grab one of them.

Two more Soldiers (Elpenor and one other) step forward.

ELPENOR

Four of us should make the run. Two and two.

POLITES

Why risk more men?

ELPENOR

He ate *two* of us last night . . .

MENETUS

He'll want another two before he sleeps . . .

ODYSSEUS

And we need him to sleep . . .

INT. SAME – LATER

A GRINDING noise as the stone is pulled back, letting daylight in. Odysseus BLINKS in the daylight as the FLOCK comes, bleating, into the cave. The silhouette of the Cyclops hangs, bent over in the entrance, looking into the cave . . .

The four Soldiers RUN, CROUCHING, against the flock . . . the Cyclops spots them, bends lower, reaching out . . . the men split left and right, RACING full bore around the Cyclops's feet – the Cyclops GRABS the two to the right in one messy grip, grinding them against the ground – at the same time he KICKS Elpenor on the left, sending him SKIDDING back along the cave floor . . . Cepheus ESCAPES . . . Elpenor SMASHES into the wall near Odysseus . . . who runs to him as the Cyclops SMASHES the two soldiers against the ground, leaving them lying there, dead, as he pulls the stone across the door, bringing darkness.

Odysseus cradles Elpenor as he dies, trying hard to block out the sound of the Cyclops FEASTING on the other two soldiers. The other Soldiers sit scattered in the dark, listening to the grim sounds . . .

INT. SAME – LATER

As the Cyclops sleeps, the soldiers silently gather around him. They pull the log from the fire, its narrow end now charred to a fine, glowing point. Odysseus gestures to them to line up opposite the massive single eye, then draws his sword and stands right by the closed eye with its WEEPING LIP-LIKE LIDS. Odysseus raises his sword, checks the line-up, then SMACKS the Cyclops's cheek with the flat of his sword – the Cyclops OPENS its EYE just in time to see – the red hot log PUNCTURES the eyeball with an awful SIZZLE –

The Cyclops ROARS and YANKS his head up, sending some of the soldiers flying into the air . . .

CYCLOPS

AHHHHRRRRAAAPPPOSSEYEEEEE . . . !!!

Odysseus RUNS for his life as the Cyclops RAGES, SCREAMING, STAMPING, WHIRLING about, BLIND and in AGONY . . . men and sheep are CRUSHED and KICKED at random.

INT. SAME – LATER

Odysseus watches his men TIE sheaves of STRAW to their bodies. He glances at the HUGE MOUND of the Cyclops, sitting with its back to the fire, SOBBING . . .

Odysseus moves to Elpenor's body. Says goodbye . . .

ANCHIALUS

What about his body?

ODYSSEUS

What about it?

ANCHIALUS

We just leave him here to rot? As food for that thing?

PHEMIUS

We honour our dead, Odysseus.

ODYSSEUS

He died helping us escape. Honour him by escaping.

Odysseus takes Elpenor's RING.

Odysseus, hearing something, looks at the Cyclops. Whose SOBS resemble WORDS . . .

CYCLOPS

MMMMPOSEIDON, FFFATHER, THEY BBBBBBBBLINDED ME. VVVENGEANCE, FFATHER. VVVVVENGEANCE . . . FOR PPPPPPPAIN . . .

One of Odysseus's men is at his side –

POLITES

It can talk. Why didn't it talk before?

ODYSSEUS

Do you talk to ants?

POLITES

Should we reason with it?

ODYSSEUS

I think that time has passed.

INT. SAME – MORNING

Odysseus and his soldiers hold three sheep each, tied together, waiting silently for the Cyclops to stir. The Cyclops RISES, feeling for the rock. Pulls it back, dazzling sheep and Soldiers with BRIGHT morning light . . . the goats, rams and sheep head, BLEATING, for the entrance . . . the Cyclops puts his hands down beside his body to feel the backs of the flock as they exit. The Soldiers climb below the sheep and PULL THEMSELVES up into the belly of the middle sheep . . .

They pass below the GIANT FINGERTIPS one by one . . . Odysseus is last, clinging to a ram as it passes beneath the Cyclops.

EXT. CAVE, ISLAND – MOMENTS LATER

Eurylochus welcomes the Soldiers as they quietly get to their feet. The Cyclops pulls the stone across the cave mouth. The Cyclops turns, its eye tight shut, wiping blood from its mouth. It SPITS . . .

CLANG. A wet helmet lands near Odysseus's feet . . . FURIOUS, he GRABS a bow from a Soldier . . .

EURYLOCHUS

No!

Odysseus LOOSES an arrow at the Cyclops's eye, striking near the damaged organ. The Cyclops BELLOWS, heading for the sound of the Soldiers FLEEING.

EURYLOCHUS

This way!

The Cyclops CRASHES after them through the forest, trees slowing him more than the Soldiers who RACE down the path,

TUMBLING DANGEROUSLY, glancing up through the trees at the pursuing Cyclops, SCRAMBLING down to the ship . . .

EXT. SHIP – CONTINUOUS

Some Soldiers LEAP aboard, GRABBING the oars, some wade to PUSH the ship away from shore then cling to the side or climb as the boat pulls away from shore . . .

The Cyclops BURSTS BLINDLY from the trees, STUMBLES into the water, FALLING – the crew ROWS for their lives –

SPLASH! The Cyclops falls into the water just short of the ship, its tremendous splash pushing the boat further from shore . . . Odysseus GRINS – the crew CHEERS . . .

With a CRASH the HEAD of the Cyclops emerges from the water – it's holding a BOULDER – it HURLS the boulder towards the sound of the crew . . .

The BOULDER LANDS on the ship's OARS – FLIPPING several OARSMEN off the boat – the Cyclops GRABS at them, BLINDLY . . .

EXT. ODYSSEUS'S SHIP – EVENING

Odysseus and Eurylochus watch the crew tend their wounds.

EURYLOCHUS

Why did you have to shoot that arrow?

ODYSSEUS

We lost good soldiers to that beast.

A soldier whose eyes are fixed on the deck, PERIMEDES, speaks.

PERIMEDES

That beast was Poseidon's son.

EURYLOCHUS

What?

PERIMEDES

When we put its eye out . . . I heard it cry his name.

ODYSSEUS

That thing was a monster.

POLITES

(quiet)

I heard it, too.

Everyone considers the implications.

EURYLOCHUS

Now the sea's against us.

POLITES

And the wind.

EURYLOCHUS

How do we get home with Poseidon against us?

ODYSSEUS

You can't live by omens and sacrifices.

EURYLOCHUS

You know how many times I've heard you weep, praying to Athena since Troy? Couldn't you have shown mercy?

ODYSSEUS

Take this. Wear it to remember those we couldn't bury.

Odysseus grabs Eurylochus's hand. Puts Elpenor's ring in it.

ODYSSEUS

The Gods help those who help themselves.

Odysseus looks at the OMINOUS horizon . . .

ODYSSEUS

(*V.O.*)

From that moment, every rough sea or headwind told the crew we were cursed . . .

He notices SUSPICION on the faces of his crew. Sees GRUMBLING amongst them . . .

EXT. BEACH OUTSIDE CALYPSO'S CAVE – DAY

Odysseus stares at bleached wood detritus, remembering . . .

ODYSSEUS

But where is my crew?

He see something in the sand. Picks it up. It is an old wooden LOT, NOTCHES on one side.

He looks up from the lot, disoriented. Sees his collection of planks like bleached whale bones . . .

ODYSSEUS

When will you let me see my men?

Calypso says nothing. Odysseus puts the lot into his belt.

ODYSSEUS

If I could just talk to them, they'd help me remember. It all went wrong. We were just trying to get home . . .

Calypso nods, encouraging him to remember.

ODYSSEUS

But where's home . . . ? I still don't remember anything before Troy . . . Did I have a wife . . . ? Children . . . perhaps a son . . . How long have I been here?

CALYPSO

A long time.

ODYSSEUS

If I had a son . . .

EXT. TELEMACHUS'S SHIP – DAY

Telemachus looks ahead at a PORT . . .

ODYSSEUS

(V.O.)

How old would he be, now?

TELEMACHUS

I don't know how to speak to a king.

MENTOR

You'll do fine. Keep your mouth shut. Never ask unless you're asked to ask.

EXT. PALACE OF MENELAUS – EVENING

Telemachus and Mentor approach the gates of the mighty palace. They can hear noise of feasting from within.

MENTOR

Zeus's law means they'll welcome us without knowing who we are. But if anyone asks –

Mentor reaches for Telemachus's hand – pulls off a DECORATIVE RING . . .

MENTOR

We're traders from Crete.

Telemachus hides the ring in his belt.

MENTOR

Then we'll figure out how to approach the king.

INT. PALACE OF MENELAUS – CONTINUOUS

Telemachus and Mentor step over the BEGGARS into a MAGNIFICENT, OPULENT MEGARON – GILDED, CROWDED with REVELLERS, DANCERS, BARDS . . . a STEWARD approaches . . .

STEWARD

Welcome.

MENTOR

Thank you.

He looks them up and down. Mentor looks at the crowd . . .

MENTOR

You seem to be having –

STEWARD

This way.

The Steward TURNS – they follow him through the celebration . . .

MENTOR

Where are you taking us?

STEWARD

The King insists on greeting strangers himself.

Telemachus looks at Mentor, nervous. Mentor leads as they follow the Steward up a flight of steps to a top table. A rugged, middle-aged man holds court. This is MENELAUS. He barely glances at Mentor before settling a careful eye on Telemachus.

MENELAUS

Sit.

Space is made next to Menelaus. Mentor tries to sit there –

MENELAUS

Not you. You.

Menelaus stares at Telemachus as he steps forward to sit . . .

MENELAUS

Enjoy our hospitality, as Zeus demands. Then perhaps you'll tell us who you are.

Telemachus nods thanks, nervous. Food and wine are put in front of them.

MENELAUS

You picked the right day to arrive. This is the feast of my daughter's wedding. Tomorrow she leaves to start a new life.

Menelaus looks Telemachus up and down.

MENELAUS

I'm Menelaus, brother of Agamemnon. Husband of Helen. Perhaps you've heard of Helen?

Menelaus turns to the profile of the beautiful woman (forties) sitting next to him. He lifts his hand to her chin.

MENELAUS

The face that launched a thousand ships.

He gently pulls her face around towards Telemachus . . .

MENELAUS

Now maybe just five hundred.

The other side of her face is viciously SCARRED.

MENELAUS

A lot of good men left on the battlefields of Troy for this face.

HELEN

And your brother's ambition.

She takes in Telemachus with cool eyes. Perhaps recognition.

HELEN

This one looks familiar.

Menelaus takes a drink. Studies Telemachus. Nods. Telemachus shifts under his gaze, uncomfortable . . .

MENELAUS

Ajax, Patrochlus . . . Achilles . . . all left under Trojan sand. But I don't miss any of them as much as I miss one particular warrior.

Telemachus stops eating, desperate to ask . . .

MENELAUS

The smartest of us all. Ten years we rotted on that beach.

INSERT CUT: HUNDREDS OF SHIPS, CAMPS, MEN, LINE THE BEACH . . .

Menelaus stares into the past . . .

MENELAUS

Deadlocked. Fighting amongst ourselves. Until one man saw a way . . .

INSERT CUT: a FIGURE on the shore, head down in contemplation . . .

Menelaus fixes Telemachus with a look –

MENELAUS

Odysseus.

Telemachus cannot hide his reaction completely.

INSERT CUT: THE GREAT WOODEN HORSE LISTS IN THE RISING TIDE . . .

MENELAUS

You've heard the story of the Horse?

Telemachus nods.

MENELAUS

But have you heard it from the *inside* . . . ?

EXT. BEACH AT TROY – DAY (FLASHBACK)

A WAVE crashes into the Horse. Sinon looks up at the sound of HOOVES.

Push in on the rough wooden chest of the Horse . . .

MENELAUS

(V.O.)

We were in there for days . . .

INT. INSIDE THE HORSE – DAY

Menelaus STRUGGLES to stay above RISING WATER in CLAUSTROPHOBIC DARKNESS, warriors PRESSED TOGETHER around him . . .

MENELAUS

(V.O.)

We'd squeezed in there before our ships even left . . . we lay silent in our own piss and shit. During the first two tides some drowned . . .

Odysseus hands a submerged warrior a hollow REED *to breathe through . . .*

MENELAUS

(V.O.)

Odysseus knew that not even Sinon, the soldier left behind, could know we were inside . . .

A SPEAR POINT CRASHES *through the side, near Odysseus.* BLOOD *drips from it. Odysseus leans his head to the wood beside the spear,* WEEPING *softly . . .*

SINON

(*O.S.; muffled*)

A gift. For Athena . . .

Odysseus mouths words of comfort through the wood . . . the point of the spear VANISHES. *Odysseus turns to Menelaus, nodding . . .*

The Warriors are JOLTED *as the Horse is pulled onto its side . . .*

EXT. THE PLAIN OF TROY – DAY

HUNDREDS *of Trojans pull the Horse, on its side, towards the great city's walls, using* TREE TRUNKS *as rollers, foot by painful foot . . .*

INT. INSIDE THE HORSE – CONTINUOUS

Odysseus passes a goatskin of water to Menelaus.

MENELAUS

(V.O.)

Odysseus kept us calm. Even as our dead began to smell . . .

EXT. GATES OF TROY – DAY

As the Horse is dragged into the city on its side, a Trojan Soldier jumps up onto the Horse, thrusting his SWORD *into the gaps in the planks –*

INT. INSIDE THE HORSE – CONTINUOUS

Odysseus JERKS *back as the blade of the sword* PROBES *the interior,* WITHDRAWN, THRUST *in again in a different spot – the blade* PENETRATES *the shoulder of the warrior next to Odysseus – who* CLAPS *his hand over the man's mouth, and wraps a rag around the blade which* WIPES *the blade clean as it is withdrawn . . .*

EXT. GATES OF TROY – CONTINUOUS

The Trojan Soldier checks his blade . . .

EXT. TROY – MOMENTS LATER

The Horse is DRAGGED *through the streets amidst a cheering mob . . .*

EXT. TROY – EVENING

The mighty Horse is PULLED *to its feet in front of the Temple of Athena. It stands there, rearing on its back feet, watched by the blank stare of the statue of Athena, as the people* SWARM *around it . . . fascinated . . . the* CROWD *starts* CHANTING *. . .*

CROWD

Burn it! Burn it! Burn it!

INT. INSIDE THE HORSE – CONTINUOUS

The Warriors can hear the UNNERVING *chant of the crowd . . .*

CROWD
(O.S.)
Burn it! Burn it! Burn it!

Odysseus looks at Menelaus, SMILES *and shakes his head.*

EXT. TROY – CONTINUOUS

Soldiers push the chanting crowd back down the stairs away from the Horse, protecting it from the mob . . .

TROJAN SOLDIER
It's an offering for Athena!

EXT. TROY – NIGHT

The Horse frozen in rearing stillness, stands in the darkness. Lamps flicker in the Temple of Athena . . .

INT. INSIDE THE HORSE – CONTINUOUS

Odysseus PULLS *tar-stained* ROPE *from lines along the 'hull' of the Horse . . . he turns back to check the Warriors are prepared before he wraps a tie line around his fist and pushes down on a panel beneath him . . .*

EXT. TROY – CONTINUOUS

The panel DROPS *from the belly of the Horse,* CAUGHT *by the tie line just above the ground. Followed by a* DEAD BODY, *lowered gently.*

Odysseus CLIMBS *silently from the Horse, followed by Menelaus and the dozen or so Warriors . . . Odysseus and Menelaus come behind Trojan Guards on the steps, take them out silently with daggers . . .*

Swords drawn they make their silent way through the shadows of the SLEEPING CITY *. . .*

EXT. GATES OF TROY – MOMENTS LATER

The Greek Warriors silently approach the VAST GATES *from both sides, taking out the Night Watch up on the ramparts . . .*

Odysseus PEERS *into the darkness.*

MENELAUS
(V.O.)
He'd known to wait for a moonless night on the plain of Troy . . .

He can hear the ocean . . . On Odysseus's silent signal, the lamps on the ramparts are DROPPED *over the wall, illuminating* MOVEMENT, *as if the ground itself were* SHUFFLING *towards the gates. Odysseus turns to the Warriors stationed at the doors and gives a signal. Polites and three others start to* TURN *the* HANDLES *that wind the* MASSIVE BOLTS *back, inch by inch . . .*

EXT. TROY – CONTINUOUS

A WATCHMAN *spots the bodies of the guards,* SOUNDS THE ALARM *. . .*

A SECOND WATCHMAN STARTS FURIOUSLY STRIKING *a metal sheet . . .*

Across the city, other Watchmen take up the alarm . . .

EXT. GATES OF TROY – CONTINUOUS

Odysseus hears the alarms . . . he shouts down to Polites . . .

ODYSSEUS
Hurry up!

Polites GRINDS *the bolts back . . .* SHOUTS *and* ALARMS *. . .*

EXT. TROY – CONTINUOUS

Trojan Soldiers put on helmets, run through the streets . . .

EXT. GATES OF TROY – CONTINUOUS

Odysseus races down the stairs – Elpenor hands him a bow and he starts shooting arrows through the olive trees at the approaching Trojan Soldiers . . .

ODYSSEUS

Come on!

Menelaus GRABS *the winch –*

MENELAUS

PULL! PULL!

Polites and his men STRAIN *against the handle, finally clearing the door, they* YANK *on the handles . . .*

THE GATES OF TROY ARE OPENED . . . STANDING THERE – THE MAGNIFICENT FIGURE OF AGAMEMNON . . . RIVERS OF GREEK WARRIORS FLOW AROUND HIM AS HE CONSIDERS HIS PRIZE . . .

MENELAUS
(V.O.)

But you know the rest . . .

INT. PALACE OF MENELAUS – NIGHT

Telemachus has tears running down his cheeks.

MENELAUS

Moved by *my* telling? You should hear the Bards sing it.

TELEMACHUS

I have. But they weren't there. With all of you –

HELEN

With Odysseus. Your father.

Telemachus looks at Helen. Nods. Menelaus GRABS his shoulders WARMLY –

MENELAUS

You are so like him.

TELEMACHUS

When did you last see him?

Menelaus's face falls. He releases Telemachus's shoulders.

MENELAUS

When we left Troy. The Gods gave us our righteous victory –

HELEN

Righteous?

Menelaus carries on –

MENELAUS

Our righteous victory, but didn't bless our voyages. It took me years to get home. And many didn't –

HELEN

Some did and wished they hadn't.

Menelaus looks at her.

HELEN

Tell him. Tell him about your brother. About the fate the Gods bestowed on him after your *righteous* struggle . . .

MENELAUS

No.

HELEN

About his hero's welcome . . .

MENELAUS

No.

HELEN

About how Agamemnon made it home years before us . . .

INSERT CUT: AGAMEMNON, resplendent in his DARK ARMOUR, approaches his PALACE, a GREETING PARTY outside the gates . . .

HELEN

(O.S.)

Tell him how he was welcomed by his queen, my twin sister, Clytemnestra . . .

The Queen steps forward to greet Agamemnon with a beautiful smile. This is CLYTEMNESTRA, who looks exactly like Helen, unscarred . . .

HELEN

Tell him about how –

MENELAUS

No! He's not here for news of my brother. He wants to hear about his father.

Helen backs down. Looking at her drunk husband with contempt.

MENELAUS

But I never heard any more of Odysseus after Troy.

Telemachus, INCREDULOUS, leans forward, FRUSTRATED . . .

TELEMACHUS

Nothing? From any of your men, or Agamemnon's? Or from traders? Some traveller must've –

Mentor places a calming hand on Telemachus's arm . . . Menelaus looks at Telemachus. Disappointed.

MENELAUS

You're interested in rumours, young man? You came here to ask me for gossip? Fine. Some said he'd perished. Some said he'd got richer, some poorer. Or imprisoned.

TELEMACHUS

Imprisoned?

MENELAUS
(dismissive)
What kind of prison . . .

INT. CALYPSO'S CAVE – NIGHT

Calypso pours Odysseus more wine . . .

MENELAUS
(*V.O.*)
Could hold a man like that?

CALYPSO
Tell me what you do remember. The rest will come . . .

ODYSSEUS
We were hit by storm after storm, all pushing us off course . . .

EXT. ODYSSEUS'S SHIP – DAY

Odysseus and his men fight to push through a PUNISHING HEAD WIND, the bow CRASHING through waves . . .

ODYSSEUS
(*V.O.*)
Until we were truly lost.

ODYSSEUS
PULL!

A sailor, Perimedes, COLLAPSES, dropping his oar – Odysseus JUMPS down to grab it, regaining the rhythm, muscles straining, SCREAMING into the wind –

ODYSSEUS
PULL! . . . PULL! . . .

A man on the bow is SWEPT OFF THE BOAT by a crashing wave . . .

INT. CALYPSO'S CAVE – NIGHT

ODYSSEUS

The men became more and more convinced that I'd offended Poseidon . . .

EXT. FORESTED SHORE – DAY

Odysseus's ships beach onto the sand. The men JUMP off into the shallow water, heading for the trees . . .

EXT. FORESTED SHORE – DAY

Odysseus leads his men through wind and SNOW into a dense forest of straight trees . . .

EXT. FOREST – DAY

Odysseus spots an ARMOURED FIGURE crouched at a stream, back to them. Eurylochus starts to draw his sword – Odysseus shakes his head. They approach cautiously . . .

ODYSSEUS

Hello?

The Figure RISES to its feet. It is THICKLY BUILT, and SLIGHTLY TALLER than them.

ODYSSEUS

We're here in peace . . .

The Armoured Figure slowly turns to face them . . .

It has the face of a child.

Odysseus looks at Eurylochus, unnerved . . .

The MONSTROUS CHILD starts GIGGLING.

Odysseus, now face to face, smiles . . .

ODYSSEUS

We need food. Food?

Odysseus mimes eating. Eurylochus steps forward.

EURYLOCHUS

We're hungry! Can't you understand?

The Monstrous Child stops giggling, looking from one to other.

ODYSSEUS

It's just a child.

Eurylochus looks at the Monstrous Child, appalled . . .

EURYLOCHUS

A child?

The Monstrous Child, seeing Eurylochus's expression, backs away.

EURYLOCHUS

If this is a *child* . . . what about its parents . . . ?

The Monstrous Child starts SCREAMING . . .

Odysseus and his men turn around, scanning the sea of tree trunks . . . Eurylochus tries to SHUSH the Monstrous Child . . .

Odysseus sees SHAPES emerging through the misty SNOW, LARGE SHAPES moving towards them between the tree trunks . . .

ARMOURED WARRIORS, TEN TO TWELVE FEET TALL, HELMETS FLAT LIKE BIRDS OF PREY, come towards Odysseus and his men . . . these are the LAESTRYGONIANS. A Soldier draws his sword, attempting to face off with a warrior TWICE his height, and is CUT DOWN INSTANTLY . . . Odysseus and his men RUN . . .

One of them RUNS and RUNS into the INCREASINGLY DENSE TREE TRUNKS, until he cannot pass . . . he turns back in the other direction, but the tree trunks behind are now TIGHTER AND TIGHTER together as if the diminishing perspective of the forest were, in fact, real . . . TRAPPED by the CAGE OF TRUNKS, they are STABBED by Laestrygonians through gaps in the trees . . .

Odysseus, Eurylochus and Polites find themselves surrounded by TREE TRUNKS that CIRCLE around them in OPPOSING directions . . . they look around, CONFUSED, when the Laestrygonians STRIKE . . . Odysseus and his men CROSS SWORDS as best they can with warriors TOWERING above them, RAINING DOWN BRUTAL STRIKES . . .

Odysseus HACKS a leg then TURNS, running BLIND, DESPERATE through the CIRCLING TREES . . .

He BURSTS out of the trees and into the water . . . his men follow . . . he gets onto his boat, as the other men try to PUSH THE BEACHED BOATS OFF THE SAND . . . Odysseus draws his bow, LOOSING ARROWS at the NARROW VISORS of the Laestrygonians as they WADE IMPLACABLY into the water, MOWING down the men pushing on the boats . . . Odysseus DOWNS two of them, the others ignore him as they POUND his men, BLOOD and FOAM CHURNING in the shallows . . . the men on the ship RACING to their oars and CALLING to their comrades . . .

Laestrygonians GRAB one of the ships, PULLING down on one side to SWAMP the boat and GRAB the crew, FLINGING them aside like rag dolls . . .

Odysseus's men start to row away . . .

ODYSSEUS

Wait! Wait for the others!

He aims his bow, targeting a Laestrygonian who is bearing down on Eurylochus in the shallows, SEA FLYING UP AROUND HIM . . . Odysseus shoots the Laestrygonian in the face, who STUMBLES to his knees as Eurylochus RUNS and RUNS and SWIMS . . .

Several of Odysseus's men have grabbed on to Laestrygonian warriors, riding massive shoulders and arms like BUCKING BRONCOS . . . the Laestrygonians HACK the boats to pieces . . .

Odysseus SHOOTS and SHOOTS as men, including Eurylochus, climb aboard . . . Odysseus sees that the other men and the two other ships are DOOMED, MASSACRED BY THE LAESTRYGONIANS . . .

ODYSSEUS
PULL!! PULL FOR YOUR LIVES!!!

Odysseus and Eurylochus watch the CARNAGE as the ship PUSHES out into deeper water . . . they sit on opposite sides of the ship, GASPING, HEAVING, GRIEVING . . . in shock for the losses. Odysseus looks up to see Athena sitting there on the deck. She shakes her head at him. He looks down, ASHAMED . . .

EXT. SAME – LATER

INSERT CUT: ATHENA MOVES THROUGH FIRE TOWARDS ODYSSEUS, WHO SLEEPS, BURNING . . . SHE REACHES OUT TO WAKE HIM –

Odysseus gets to his feet, surveys their distance from shore.

ODYSSEUS
Turn to port. Follow the coast.

EURYLOCHUS
We need to get as far away as possible.

Odysseus crouches beside Eurylochus, quiet . . .

ODYSSEUS
We don't have the supplies for a blind crossing. We've lost our way. We need to find food. And get our bearings.

As the men row, they WATCH Odysseus and Eurylochus. The Helmsman pulls the tiller, pointing the ship parallel to the rocky coastline . . .

EXT. ODYSSEUS'S SHIP – LATER

The weather has CALMED. Odysseus spots a plume of SMOKE from deep in the forest.

ODYSSEUS

There! Find anchorage.

Eurylochus looks at the smoke as the ship heads towards shore.

EXT. GRASSY SHORE – EVENING

Odysseus's ship drops anchor close to shore. There are other boats of various sizes abandoned on the beach. ROTTING.

ODYSSEUS

Form a landing party. A large one.

EURYLOCHUS

Tomorrow.

Odysseus looks at Eurylochus, struck by his forceful tone.

ODYSSEUS

Tomorrow.

EXT. GRASSY SHORE – DAWN

Odysseus steps out of the water, stepping past the bones of old boats, peering up the hillside. He turns to Eurylochus.

ODYSSEUS

Leave someone with the tender.

EURYLOCHUS

We think you should stay.

ODYSSEUS

We?

EURYLOCHUS

All of us. Still alive.

Odysseus looks at Eurylochus. Then at the BATTERED, DESPERATE faces of his men. None will meet his eye. He speaks softly to Eurylochus . . .

ODYSSEUS

Is this a mutiny?

EURYLOCHUS

That's up to you.

Odysseus considers. Smiles, CONFIDENT –

ODYSSEUS

Give me your bow. I'll make sure we eat tonight, whatever you find.

Odysseus heads alone into the grassy hills. Eurylochus leads the men towards the plume of smoke.

EXT. HILLS – LATER

Odysseus CREEPS through the grass, bow in hand . . . listening.

EXT. CLEARING, DERELICT TEMPLE – DAY

Eurylochus and the men climb a path through a series of RUINS. At one end a ROUGH STONE HOUSE, smoke coming from the chimney. They make their way towards it. A Soldier spots something in an abandoned doorway . . . a LION, staring at them. The Soldier pulls his bow, Eurylochus RESTRAINS him. They move closer to the lion, which has seen them, but just sits there. Eurylochus looks around them, realizing that OTHER PREDATORY ANIMALS are staring at them from the ruined structures – WOLVES, LEOPARDS – all calmly watching the Soldiers. TAME.

Eurylochus cautiously approaches the stone house . . .

EXT. HILLS – CONTINUOUS

Odysseus HEARS the crack of a twig. He PEERS through the leaves . . .

EXT. STONE HOUSE – CONTINUOUS

Eurylochus slowly, cautiously, crosses the threshold . . .

INT. STONE HOUSE – CONTINUOUS

He peers into the gloom . . . watched by a CROW in a CAGE. A long table. A large fire. A bubbling pot. Hanging poultry and dressed meats. It smells amazing to desperate men . . .

A SCREAM – a TERRIFIED WOMAN at the back door DROPS her milk pail in TERROR at the sight of strange Soldiers in her house – she BOLTS out the back – the Crow in the cage SQUAWKS –

EURYLOCHUS

Wait!

He runs after her . . .

EXT. HILLS – DAY

Odysseus spies a magnificent, proud BUCK, chewing on leaves . . . he gingerly strings his bow. Draws an arrow. But can't resist PLUCKING the taut string – the buck BOLTS – Odysseus gives chase, bow in hand . . .

EXT. BACK OF STONE HOUSE – DAY

Eurylochus GRABS the woman, who SCREAMS again . . .

EURYLOCHUS

It's alright. It's okay.

She stops screaming, looking at Eurylochus, TERRIFIED.

EURYLOCHUS

It's okay. I'm not going to hurt you. No one's going to hurt you.

WOMAN

(sobbing)

If I do what you want.

Eurylochus shakes his head.

EURYLOCHUS

No one's going to hurt you. My name is Eurylochus. What's your name?

The woman's breathing slows . . .

WOMAN

Circe.

EURYLOCHUS

Circe, we need food. Badly.

CIRCE

I have food. Lots of food.

EXT. HILLS – DAY

Odysseus CHASES the buck – stops – LOOSES a shot – MISSES . . .

INT. STONE HOUSE – DAY

Eurylochus and the men CROWD the table, watching Circe stir the pot like hungry dogs, studying her every move.

CIRCE

Your weapons. Your armour. You can put them out the back . . .

The Crow in the Cage watches them watch her as they start to peel off their armour . . .

EXT. STONE HOUSE – MOMENTS LATER

Perimedes carries armour out the back door. As he drops it he notices some OLD ARMOUR, half buried in SNOW, weeds growing through it . . . a graveyard of armour to match the graveyard of boats at the beach . . . He heads back inside as others drops their armour outside.

EXT. HILLS – DAY

Odysseus SHOOTS – the arrow sticks in the buck's leg – it runs, limping . . .

INT. STONE HOUSE – DAY

As Circe DISHES STEW, the RAVENOUS MEN STUFF THEIR FACES . . .

EXT. HILLS – DAY

Odysseus gains ground on the injured buck . . .

INT. STONE HOUSE – DAY

The men CHOMP AND EAT AND SLURP AND BURP AND EAT AND EAT –

Circe sits down next to Eurylochus, watching him GORGE HIMSELF.

CIRCE

You like my meat?

Eurylochus NODS, tries to talk through his MANIC FEASTING –

EURYLOCHUS

Why – do – have – so – much – ?

Eating so hard he can't breathe. Circe smiles.

CIRCE

You never know when strangers will come . . .

EXT. HILLS – CONTINUOUS

Odysseus draws back his bow and SHOOTS, hitting the buck square in the chest . . . he watches it DROP into the undergrowth . . .

INT. STONE HOUSE – CONTINUOUS

Circe reaches out to touch Eurylochus's hair . . .

CIRCE

Men. With their appetites . . .

Eurylochus notices her STROKING his head, but nothing can stop him eating . . .

CIRCE

Too much is never enough . . .

She is FIRMLY RUBBING his head as if he were a dog . . .

EXT. HILLS – CONTINUOUS

Odysseus approaches the spot where the buck fell. He sees something strange in the undergrowth . . .

INT. STONE HOUSE – CONTINUOUS

Circe RUBS her hand over Eurylochus's ear – it POPS up the other side of her hand POINTED and HAIRY . . . a PIG'S EAR –

The Crow in the cage SQUAWKS and JUMPS up and down –

EXT. HILLS – CONTINUOUS

Odysseus looks down, SHOCKED. Where the buck fell is a NAKED MAN, Odysseus's ARROW IN HIS CHEST . . .

Odysseus looks up –

INT. STONE HOUSE – CONTINUOUS

Circe RUBS Eurylochus's head with both hands, the dark hair becoming LIGHT and BRISTLY in the wake of each STROKE . . .

The other men notice but MUST KEEP EATING, as if THE FOOD IS EATING THEM, PULLING THEIR HANDS DOWN, THEN PUSHING THEM, LADEN, INTO THEIR UNWILLING FACES . . .

Circe spreads her hands across Eurylochus's face, MASSAGING his cheeks – as her hands SPREAD APART they reveal a SNOUT . . .

EXT. HILLS – CONTINUOUS

Odysseus SPRINTS down the hill –

ODYSSEUS

Eurylochus! EURYLOCHUS!

INT. STONE HOUSE – CONTINUOUS

As PIGS squirm across the floor, Circe SLAPS an eating Soldier's face – leaving a PIG'S FACE in its place . . .

EXT. GRASSY SHORE – EVENING

Odysseus BURSTS from the trees to confront Antiphates, standing watch.

ODYSSEUS

Where are they?!

Antiphates looks at him, confused.

ANTIPHATES

They haven't come back.

ODYSSEUS

None of them?

ANTIPHATES

No.

Odysseus looks up at the smoke, thinking.

ODYSSEUS

Give me your dagger. And sword.

He takes Antiphates' weapons, hiding the dagger in his shin guards and the sword across his back. Then heads up the hillside towards the smoke . . .

EXT. DERELICT TEMPLE – EVENING

Odysseus climbs up through the ruins. Watching the stone house. With its sty FULL OF PIGS. In front of him is a TAME LION . . . Odysseus crouches by the lion, reaching out to its mane, looking deep into its SAD EYES . . .

He hears the DOOR OPEN, looks over to the house to see Circe emerge with a bucket of SLOPS for the pigs. Odysseus watches her DUMP the slops into the sty . . . she LOOKS UP, sensing him –

CIRCE

Why don't you come out?

Odysseus steps forward. Circe looks him up and down.

CIRCE

Have you come from the sea?

Odysseus nods.

CIRCE

Are you alone?

Odysseus nods again, stepping cautiously closer. The pigs see him and CROWD around, SNIFFING at him, POKING him with their snouts . . . Circe LAUGHS –

CIRCE

My pigs have taken a liking to you. Are you hungry?

Odysseus nods.

CIRCE

Leave your weapons at the door and enjoy the hospitality of Zeus.

He pulls his swords and bow and rests them against the wall.

CIRCE

Grab a hog. You can slaughter it for your dinner.

Odysseus looks at the pigs, crowded around his legs. Splits one from the others and pushes it inside . . . as he shuts the door he looks out at the remaining pigs, STARING at him. They start SQUEALING. He shuts the door.

INT. STONE HOUSE – CONTINUOUS

The pig runs, SQUEALING, into the gloomy kitchen, hiding in a corner. Circe hands Odysseus a CLEAVER, pointing to the back door . . . the Crow in the Cage SQUAWKS.

Odysseus moves to the pig, which PANICS. Circe watches Odysseus struggle to control the pig.

CIRCE

Whoever you are, you're clearly not a farmer. Here –

She reaches for the cleaver. Odysseus puts the cleaver down by the fire, letting the pig go.

ODYSSEUS

The stew smells good. That's plenty for just us.

CIRCE

Who says it's just us?

ODYSSEUS

Who else is here?

CIRCE

Who, indeed?

Circe scoops some stew from the bubbling pot into a bowl and puts it on the table.

CIRCE

You say you're alone.

She drops a lump of bread next to the bowl. Odysseus sits.

CIRCE

But no one comes here alone.

ODYSSEUS

No?

Odysseus examines the CHUNKS of PINK MEAT . . . Circe sits next to him.

CIRCE

You can only reach this spot by sea . . .

She pours them both dark red wine from a jug.

CIRCE

So where are your shipmates?

Odysseus picks up his cup, looking at the dark liquid.

ODYSSEUS

I'm looking for them. Has anyone come this way?

Circe looks at him. Gulps at her wine, leaving red across her lips and chin. She shakes her head. The Crow in the cage SQUAWKS.

ODYSSEUS

But you had all this food prepared.

CIRCE

You're questioning me? You? A traveller who's clearly starving, but hasn't touched the food in front of him. Who claims to be a sailor but wears a Greek warrior's armour. Who breaks Zeus's law by bringing a dagger into his hostess's house.

ODYSSEUS

You've got sharp eyes.

CIRCE

Sharpened by the Gods.

ODYSSEUS

They grant you insights?

CIRCE

Truths. Sometimes.

The pigs are SQUEALING at the door . . .

ODYSSEUS

Would they tell you where my men are?

CIRCE

Your men? You command them?

Odysseus nods. Circe thinks.

CIRCE

Yes, they would.

ODYSSEUS

Would you tell me?

CIRCE

Perhaps. If you give me your dagger.

Odysseus reaches down, produces the dagger. Hands it to her.

CIRCE

But why would I help a liar who refuses my hospitality?

Odysseus picks up his cup. SIPS, giving himself red lips.

CIRCE

Your men were here earlier.

The pigs HAMMER the door . . .

CIRCE

Now they're not.

Odysseus takes a forkful of pink meat, raises it to his mouth – the Crow in the Cage SQUAWKS and SQUAWKS – Odysseus pauses – Circe THROWS a chunk of bread at the bars of the cage, silencing it. Odysseus SPOTS SOMETHING in the bread bowl . . .

The pigs are SQUEALING, THROWING themselves against the door –

ODYSSEUS

They moved on?

Odysseus reaches for the bread bowl as Circe brings the dagger above the table . . .

CIRCE

Yes.

He turns the bowl over letting a RING RATTLE onto the table – the ring he gave Eurylochus.

ODYSSEUS

Leaving their rings?

The Pigs BURST THROUGH THE DOOR –

Odysseus SMASHES his hand through the bars of the Crow's cage –

Circe brings the dagger to Odysseus's throat –

ODYSSEUS

I wouldn't . . .

Circe looks to where Odysseus's hand HAS THE CROW BY THE THROAT. She freezes – the PIGS SURROUND THEM, SQUEALING –

CIRCE

DON'T!

ODYSSEUS

I don't know who this crow is to you, but if you don't put the knife down I'll throttle it to find out.

Circe drops the dagger.

CIRCE

Don't hurt her!

Odysseus looks from Circe to the crow and back.

ODYSSEUS

Family? Mother? Your sister?

Circe nods. The PIGS push their snouts against her with increasing violence –

ODYSSEUS

You turned her into this like you turned my men into pigs –

CIRCE

I didn't turn your men into anything! This is who they are. Look at them –

Odysseus looks at the SQUEALING, WRITHING PIGS –

CIRCE

Base. Disgusting, primal urges you value in battle . . . they've raped and pillaged across the world for you – you think that's against their nature? You think they only did those things because you ordered them to?

Odysseus tries not to look at the pigs. Circe sees his discomfort.

CIRCE

A true commander thinks his men's savagery is actually discipline. You don't seem that deluded. But you sent them to me, here, on my own. A gang of filthy soldiers with empty bellies and hot blood. You thought they'd respect me and my home? Look at them. Know your own men.

Odysseus looks from the pigs to Circe. Tightens his grip on her Crow.

ODYSSEUS

Did they hurt you?

CIRCE

They would've.

ODYSSEUS

They just want to go home. Let them.

Circe looks at Odysseus. At her Caged Crow. She puts her knife down . . .

CIRCE

Let her go.

Odysseus gently releases the crow, which SQUAWKS. Circe RUBS her hands together and GRABS a pig, RUBBING human life back into it as if trying to warm it up, STREAK by STREAK, FUR FALLS . . .

CIRCE

Come back. Back into your disguises . . .

Men EMERGE from her hands as if from sleep, NAKED, DISORIENTED, ANGRY . . .

ODYSSEUS

Where are their clothes?

Circe nods at the back door as she works her magic . . .

INT. SAME – LATER

Odysseus's men are dressed, standing at one end of the room.

Odysseus picks up Eurylochus's ring and TOSSES it to him.

ODYSSEUS

Back to the ship.

GRATEFUL and OBEDIENT, the men file past Odysseus on their way out, murmuring thanks.

ODYSSEUS

Take all the food you can carry. Not the meat.

The men leave. Eurylochus comes close –

EURYLOCHUS

You're not going to let her live? She's a witch!

ODYSSEUS

Who gave her powers? Your Gods. Fill the jugs and skins at the stream and prepare to sail at dawn.

Eurylochus nods. Odysseus and Circe are alone. Odysseus indicates the crow –

ODYSSEUS

Why leave her like this?

CIRCE

We get on better this way.

Odysseus gently places his dagger back in his shin guard.

ODYSSEUS

I'm sorry if we offended you.

Circe says nothing.

ODYSSEUS

We can't leave without your help. We need bearings. We need to know the way back to the trade routes.

Circe looks at him with insight. Judges.

CIRCE

You're too lost.

ODYSSEUS

What do you mean?

CIRCE

Only blind Tiresias can tell you how to go home.

ODYSSEUS

Tiresias?

CIRCE

In Hades.

Odysseus stares at her.

ODYSSEUS

Nobody sails into hell and comes back.

CIRCE

You will . . .

EXT. ODYSSEUS'S SHIP – TWILIGHT

Odysseus PEERS ahead into the DARKENING MIST . . .

CIRCE

(V.O.)

If you head north in the twilight . . .

A BLACK, ROCKY SHORE looms out of the mist. Dead trees. Volcanic rock. Obsidian beaches . . .

INT. STONE HOUSE – NIGHT

CIRCE

Head inland until a river of fire meets a river of ice . . .

EXT. HADES – TWILIGHT

Odysseus leads his men, with a RAM and EWE, across a BLACK, DEAD LANDSCAPE . . .

To a place where a river of WHITE-HOT LAVA flows down to meet a GLACIER tumbling into the STEAMING sea . . .

CIRCE

(V.O.)

There you must dig a trench . . .

Odysseus, using his sword, digs a trench in the black sand . . .

CIRCE

(V.O.)

Fill it with the blood of sacrifice to gather the dead . . .

Odysseus's men SLAUGHTER the ram and ewe, BLEEDING them into the trench, then setting a fire behind Odysseus who sits at the trench of blood, peering into the darkness . . .

INT. STONE HOUSE – NIGHT

CIRCE

And learn how you go home.

Odysseus nods thanks. He turns to leave –

CIRCE

You.

He turns back.

CIRCE

Not your men.

ODYSSEUS

You'd curse them?

Circe shakes her head.

CIRCE

Not a curse – a truth. Your men don't want you to defy the Gods. But the Gods say only you make it home.

ODYSSEUS

Then I defy the Gods.

Odysseus turns and leaves.

EXT. HADES – TWILIGHT

Odysseus looks uneasy as he sees the black, gravelly sand start to MOVE . . . SHAPES emerge from the ground . . . SHADES of the dead, DIGGING their way out into the FLICKERING FIRELIGHT . . . the Shades SHUFFLE forwards, approaching the blood, black in the twilight and firelight . . .

Odysseus uses his sword to stop the Shades from drinking the blood . . . he recognizes a Shade –

ODYSSEUS

Sinon?

The Shade ignores him, fixated on the blood . . . Odysseus leans down to look at his face – it is Sinon, the Greek Soldier left behind with the Wooden Horse at Troy.

ODYSSEUS

Sinon, it's Odysseus.

ELDERLY VOICE

(O.S.)

Let him drink.

Odysseus TURNS. An old man with BANDAGED EYES crouches by the blood. This is TIRESIAS. He SCOOPS blood into his mouth. It glistens black on his chin . . .

TIRESIAS

Then you'll hear his testament.

Odysseus lifts his sword away from between Sinon and the blood . . . Sinon, parched, gulps black bubbling blood.

ODYSSEUS

Sinon?

Sinon looks at Odysseus, recognizing him.

SINON

Odysseus. You lied to everyone. Did you have to lie to me?

ODYSSEUS

I needed you to believe.

EXT. BEACH AT TROY – DAY (FLASHBACK)

Odysseus talks privately with Sinon. Beached ships and the Horse under construction in the background . . .

ODYSSEUS

Why did you have to volunteer?

Sinon smiles at Odysseus.

SINON

Don't you remember how I came here?

ODYSSEUS

Yes.

INSERT CUT: Teenage Sinon and Teenage Antinous stand at the head of the lottery line. Eumaeus waves Odysseus over. Antinous shows him his lot . . .

SINON

I begged to take Antinous's place. He'd been called, but –

ODYSSEUS

He offered money for your family if you'd take his place. You begged me to let you go so Antinous would take care of your father . . .

Odysseus listens to Teenage Sinon's plea. Takes the lot from Antinous and hands it to Sinon . . .

ODYSSEUS

So I did.

Odysseus turns Antinous away, giving him back to his father . . .

Sinon reaches into his belt . . .

SINON

If the Trojans don't let me live. If I never make it home . . .

Pulls out the LOT.

SINON

Take this back to my father. Tell him everything I did.

Odysseus takes the lot, starts to leave –

SINON

Odysseus?

ODYSSEUS

Yes?

SINON

Feel free to add some stuff.

Odysseus smiles sadly at this . . .

EXT. HADES – TWILIGHT (PRESENT)

Sinon's bloody-chinned shade looks accusingly at Odysseus.

SINON

You didn't trust me with the truth? After all those years? I was a boy when I came with you to Troy. You knew I'd die for you.

ODYSSEUS

Dying men tell the truth. I needed you to believe.

SINON

I died for your lie on that beach.

ODYSSEUS

I know. I was there with you.

INSERT CUT: ODYSSEUS, tearful, leans his head against the wood, next to the bloody spear point inside the Wooden Horse.

ODYSSEUS

I heard you repeat my lie with your dying breath. Winning us the war. I was right there. Inches from you. Smelling your blood.

SINON

What comfort could that give me? Not knowing you were inside that Horse until the dead told me.

ODYSSEUS

Which dead?

Sinon gestures to the HORDES of Shades on the obsidian plain.

SINON

A lot of veterans of your campaigns walk these shores. The dead meet to lament the living and greet the newly dead. My father was the first Shade to find me.

ODYSSEUS

To comfort you?

SINON

Shades don't comfort. They want word of the living who wronged them. My father had died in poverty, alone, begging for scraps from people like Antinous.

ODYSSEUS

Antinous cheated you?

SINON

As he's no doubt cheating you.

ODYSSEUS

How?

SINON

Who's in Ithaca looking after your wife and son?

ODYSSEUS

My wife is not a concern.

SINON

Nor was my father. Talk to Agamemnon about homecomings.

ODYSSEUS

Agamemnon's here?

Sinon nods. Steps back from the blood.

SINON

You buried me at Troy with respect. Thank you. But spare a thought for those you didn't.

ODYSSEUS

It's not always possible.

SINON

Honour your fallen, Odysseus. When you get home, take a ship, head into the unknown west till you find land . . . there, give sacrifice and honour your men.

Odysseus nods. Sinon turns to go, then STOPS –

SINON

Do you still have the lot?

Odysseus reaches into his belt, pulls out the lot.

ODYSSEUS

Of course.

SINON

If you make it home . . . give Antinous back his shame.

ODYSSEUS

I will.

Sinon moves into the crowd of Shades. Odysseus sees one plume of a grand helmet stand above all others. The Shade of Agamemnon approaches.

ODYSSEUS

My Lord.

Agamemnon crouches to drink, removing his mighty helmet . . . he looks up at Odysseus with bloody chin and dark eyes.

AGAMEMNON

Odysseus. You're not here.

ODYSSEUS

Not yet.

AGAMEMNON

But you're not home?

ODYSSEUS

Not yet. How are *you* here? We won the war, you headed for home . . .

AGAMEMNON

Odysseus. Most brilliant of all my generals. You would never be snared as I was.

ODYSSEUS

Were you cast adrift like us?

AGAMEMNON

No. My misfortune was to make it home.

INSERT CUT: AGAMEMNON is greeted outside his vast palace by CLYTEMNESTRA at the head of the household . . .

AGAMEMNON

(V.O.)

To be welcomed by my beautiful wife . . .

Clytemnestra directs servants who pull Agamemnon's armour from his body. Bathe, anoint and prepare him for bed.

Agamemnon's dark-eyed Shade remembers . . .

AGAMEMNON

(V.O.)

Bathed, anointed. Made soft.

INT. AGAMEMNON'S BEDCHAMBER – EVENING

Agamemnon lies back on the cushions of his bed. Clytemnestra approaches, kneeling before him with downturned, modest gaze. She opens her robe as she moves towards her husband . . .

AGAMEMNON

(V.O.)

To learn the hardest lesson. I'd left poison in her heart years before . . .

INSERT CUT: Agamemnon carries a SCREAMING ADOLESCENT GIRL towards a STORMY SEA . . . watched by an AGONIZED Clytemnestra . . .

AGAMEMNON

(V.O.)

The good part of her heart had gone to another. Leaving me the blackened, rotten remains . . .

In a flash, CLYTEMNESTRA LEAPS FORWARD, STABBING AGAMEMNON UP THROUGH THE CHIN –

EXT. HADES – TWILIGHT

AGAMEMNON

She and her lover had plotted my murder for years. Odysseus?

ODYSSEUS

Yes?

AGAMEMNON

My son, Orestes. Did he avenge me?

ODYSSEUS

My Lord, how could I know? I'm still trying to get home.

AGAMEMNON

Don't make my mistake. Don't walk in the front door expecting garlands and praise. Come in disguise. Take your time. Assess.

Odysseus watches Agamemnon rise. Melt into the Shades. Tiresias turns to look at Odysseus with blind eyes.

TIRESIAS

Do you see?

ODYSSEUS

I understand what I have to do.

TIRESIAS

Some of what you have to do.

Tiresias indicates Eurylochus and the other men.

TIRESIAS

My prophecy isn't for their ears.

Eurylochus and the men move back towards the ship . . .

TIRESIAS

Sail southwest past the Sirens. Their song lures your men onto the rocks. They all die.

ODYSSEUS

I won't let that happen. I'll block their ears. With wax.

TIRESIAS

Past the Sirens you choose between the whirlpool Charybdis and the monster Scylla. The whirlpool in the sea would take *all* your lives, the monster in the cliffs only *six*. But your determination to sacrifice no more lives kills all of them.

ODYSSEUS

I'll do what I have to.

TIRESIAS

At the end. When starvation and mutiny threaten, they demand to land where the Sun God's cattle graze. They slaughter Apollo's herd. Zeus kills them for it. Do you see?

ODYSSEUS

I'll stop them.

TIRESIAS

Why do these lives matter more to you than those you've already lost?

Tiresias gestures back at the Shades.

ODYSSEUS

I can still save them from the Gods.

TIRESIAS

But not from themselves.

A STIRRING catches Odysseus's attention – AGITATION amongst the Shades heads across the plain towards him . . .

ODYSSEUS

Who are they?

TIRESIAS

Your unburied crew. Demanding you share their dishonour . . .

Odysseus gets to his feet, calling to his men –

ODYSSEUS

Let's go!

They RUN towards the ship, as the Shades of Odysseus's crew SCRAMBLE across the black plain towards them, GAINING and GAINING . . . Odysseus and his men cast off as the HISSING, PATHETIC SHADES reach the shore, MOANING for justice . . . Odysseus's crew look at them, appalled as they row –

ODYSSEUS

Pull!

The rower across from Eurylochus talks excitedly, scared –

ROWERS

I saw Sinon! I saw Elpenor! Is that our fate?!

Eurylochus, straining with effort, GLARES at the men –

EURYLOCHUS

Shut up and pull!

Odysseus, at the helm, looks back at the dwindling haunted black shore . . .

ODYSSEUS

(V.O.)

We rowed out of hell . . .

INT. CALYPSO'S CAVE – NIGHT

Odysseus rubs his face with his hands . . .

ODYSSEUS

Leaving so many fallen comrades . . . I have to save the rest . . .

Calypso touches his forearm. He looks up, CONCERNED –

ODYSSEUS

Where are they? Are they here? What's happened to them?! Did they leave me here?! Are they coming back?!

Odysseus turns his gaze on Calypso, MANIC –

ODYSSEUS

Did you do something to them?!

Calypso shushes him gently, offers him a dish . . .

CALYPSO

Have some.

Odysseus looks down at the lotus flower, suddenly quiet . . .

ODYSSEUS

You told me not to eat the lotus flower.

CALYPSO

Just tonight. To help you sleep. Think no more of your crew. Sleep. Tomorrow, when you're ready, you'll remember . . . your crew, your family . . .

Odysseus wolfs down the lotus . . . pauses . . . calming . . .

ODYSSEUS

Family . . . a wife . . .

INT. PENELOPE'S CHAMBER, PALACE OF ITHACA – DAY

Penelope at her loom, patiently WEAVES the burial shroud . . .

ODYSSEUS

(V.O.)

Do I have a wife?

Antinous steps past the screen into the chamber. Penelope looks at him, surprised. Her Maid, Melantho, tries to stop him approaching.

PENELOPE

It's alright, Melantho.

Antinous steps forward . . .

PENELOPE

Strangers don't come in here.

ANTINOUS

Screen or no screen, after three years of feasting together we're far from strangers, Penelope.

PENELOPE

Do you want to marry me, or ruin my reputation?

Antinous nods at Melantho.

ANTINOUS

Melantho can be discreet.

He looks over Penelope's shoulder at her work . . .

ANTINOUS

And I'm actually here out of concern for your reputation.

PENELOPE

Oh?

ANTINOUS

Everybody sees how hard you work.

PENELOPE

Slow, steady progress.

ANTINOUS

But, every night, you've been unravelling that work.

Penelope turns to Melantho. Hard.

PENELOPE

So much for discretion.

(to Melantho)

Leave us.

Antinous watches Melantho go. They exchange a look as she passes . . .

ANTINOUS

You can't expect her to be loyal to a master she never even knew.

PENELOPE

I expect her to be loyal to me.

ANTINOUS

And she will be, when you're married to me. Slaves have no choice but to be loyal to the future. This is a household waiting for a master, just as Ithaca's a kingdom waiting for a king.

PENELOPE

Ithaca's king is coming back.

ANTINOUS

No. He's not.

He moves closer, to speak more discreetly.

ANTINOUS

Did you know that as a boy I tried to go with him to Troy?

PENELOPE

He never told me that.

ANTINOUS

I tried to take the place of our shepherd's son. Odysseus refused to let me. He knew that Ithaca needed a future without him, and he saw me as part of that future.

Antinous picks up the threads of the shroud, tugging, experimentally.

ANTINOUS

I'll never tell the other Suitors about your deception. But finish your weaving. It's time to let him go.

Penelope studies Antinous . . .

PENELOPE

Why would you want to marry someone who loves somebody else?

ANTINOUS

Your loyalty to Odysseus is one of your finest qualities.

Antinous looks into her eyes.

ANTINOUS

I love you. I want you to choose me, and end all this. Don't tell me you're not tired. The waiting, the uncertainty. You've done your duty year after year after year. It's time to think of yourself. It's time to live again . . . it's what Odysseus would've wanted.

Penelope looks back at him. Exhausted. Tempted.

ANTINOUS

I'll take care of all your needs, my Queen.

He gently reaches towards her face . . .

PENELOPE

And my son?

ANTINOUS

The throne is his. He's the heir.

Antinous brushes a strand of hair from her face . . .

ANTINOUS

Unless we have a child of our own.

Too much. Penelope turns back to her work, ashamed.

ANTINOUS

Where *is* Telemachus?

PENELOPE

He went inland to see his grandfather.

INT. MEGARON, PALACE OF ITHACA – MOMENTS LATER

Eumaeus hears Antinous come down the steps in the empty hall . . . Melantho steps from the shadows. Antinous goes to her, the intimacy between them apparent.

MELANTHO

She's lying. He's gone to sea.

EXT. COURTYARD, PALACE OF ITHACA – CONTINUOUS

Antinous comes out into a half dozen of the Suitors.

ANTINOUS

He's gone for news of his father . . .

INT. MEGARON, PALACE OF ITHACA – CONTINUOUS

Eumaeus shuffles towards the door to hear what the Suitors are discussing . . .

EXT. COURTYARD, PALACE OF ITHACA – CONTINUOUS

Antinous thinks. Realizes.

ANTINOUS

He's gone to Sparta. To Menelaus.

POLYBUS

Should we go there?

Antinous thinks.

ANTINOUS

No.

INT. MEGARON, PALACE OF ITHACA – CONTINUOUS

Eumaeus hears SPURS approaching – he turns . . .

EUMAEUS

Too loud, Melanthius. I told you, you're a cowherd –

Melanthius GRABS him by the arm – pulls him through the door –

EXT. COURTYARD, PALACE OF ITHACA – CONTINUOUS

Melanthius PUSHES Eumaeus into the light.

MELANTHIUS

He was listening.

Antinous turns, looking at Eumaeus.

EUMAEUS

I was coming for Argus –

Eumaeus waves in the direction of the dung pile. Argus lies on it, half-dead.

ANTINOUS

I told you, that dog stays there. Go back to the farm. When we need your pigs we'll send Melanthius. You're no longer welcome in this palace.

Eumaeus straightens up, trying for some dignity.

EUMAEUS

I answer to my mistress.

ANTINOUS

Does she even know your name, old man?

Tears appear in Eumaeus's eyes . . . Antinous takes pity.

ANTINOUS

If she asks for you, we'll send word. Now go.

Eumaeus, refusing Melanthius's help, makes his way out of the courtyard. Antinous turns to Polybus.

ANTINOUS

Telemachus will come back by the temple at Pylos. Take your man and wait for him there.

POLYBUS

While you stay here, trying to charm the queen? I don't think so.

ANTINOUS

Telemachus needs to die on the road.

Polybus signals a BEGGAR sitting by the wall. He approaches.

POLYBUS

Irus has a plan.

IRUS nods at Antinous.

IRUS

Telemachus and his men will be ready for the Bandits who work the road between here and Pylos. But if some of them took the temple from the priests before they arrived . . .

Antinous considers this. Nods. To Irus –

ANTINOUS

No witnesses – everyone in that party dead in a ditch, throats open. Bring me part of Telemachus as proof. His nose.

POLYBUS

Would you know him from his nose?

ANTINOUS

Ears, too, then.

EXT. OLIVE GROVE, SPARTA – DAY

Helen and her MAIDS watch as Telemachus HUNTS with Menelaus. Menelaus watches, approving, as Telemachus WHIPS his bow up, shooting a bird mid-flight.

MENELAUS

Who taught you to hunt?

TELEMACHUS

My father's swineherd.

MENELAUS

His swineherd?

TELEMACHUS

His most loyal servant.

Menelaus laughs –

MENELAUS

Of course he'd leave his most loyal man behind. He was always the smartest. The only one Agamemnon ever listened to. He should've listened harder.

TELEMACHUS

Can I ask . . . What happened to your brother?

Menelaus starts DRESSING the bird . . .

MENELAUS

His wife betrayed him. When he returned from Troy, she and her lover murdered him. Years before I made it home.

TELEMACHUS

What did you do to them?

MENELAUS

His son, Orestes, had already killed them both.

TELEMACHUS

(appalled)

He killed his own mother?

Menelaus looks at Telemachus, hard.

MENELAUS

He avenged his father.

Telemachus nods uncertainly . . . Menelaus GRINS –

MENELAUS

Don't worry, your mother has nothing in common with Clytemnestra.

TELEMACHUS

Maybe not, but the suitors have convinced the Elders she needs to remarry.

MENELAUS

It's a bad time for an empty throne. You've heard stories of the people from the sea?

TELEMACHUS

Have you been raided?

MENELAUS

Not yet. But the attacks seem to be getting closer. Sparta's ready. How will Ithaca raise an army to defend itself?

TELEMACHUS

Someone has to take the throne.

MENELAUS

Then the battle's there, not here. You've run away from the problem.

Telemachus looks hard at Menelaus. Who shakes his head.

MENELAUS

And you've left your mother at the mercy of those suitors.

TELEMACHUS

Should I hire mercenaries? Go back and kill them all?

MENELAUS

Murder the rich and powerful guests in your house? You'd be exiled.

TELEMACHUS

What, then?

MENELAUS

You have to evict them without violating Zeus's law.

TELEMACHUS

(understanding)

I have to take the throne. I need to know Odysseus's fate . . .

MENELAUS

This isn't about a father you've never known. You have to lead . . .

EXT. BEACH OUTSIDE CALYPSO'S CAVE – DAY

Odysseus pulls a weathered piece of wooden railing from the sand.

MENELAUS

(V.O.)

Whatever's happened to Odysseus.

He stares at a round knob on the top . . .

INSERT CUT: *in a fearsome night-time* STORM, *Odysseus* CLINGS *to the knob . . .*

Calypso watches as Odysseus carries the railing up the beach and lays it next to a row of planks he's collected.

CALYPSO

You need to remember.

Odysseus looks up at her with fearful eyes . . .

ODYSSEUS

No, I don't. I don't want to know the truth. I'm happy here with you.

CALYPSO

Then why are you gathering the bones of your old ship for a raft?

Odysseus looks down at the BLEACHED WOOD, laid out in a square pattern, realizing for the first time what he's been doing . . .

CALYPSO

Remember. Remember your crew. Your journey. After Hades . . . did you pass the Sirens?

ODYSSEUS

The Sirens. Yes.

INSERT CUT: *the Crew put* BEESWAX *into their ears, supervised by Odysseus . . .*

Odysseus turns to Calypso, remembering, a tear appears in his eye as he marvels –

ODYSSEUS

I heard the song of the Sirens . . .

And the sound of TUNEFUL WIND takes us –

EXT. ODYSSEUS'S SHIP AMONGST ROCKY ISLANDS – DAY

Odysseus's ship moves into a FIELD of SMALL ROCKY ISLANDS . . . Odysseus peers from rock to rock . . .

Odysseus hears the sound of the wind. Gestures to Eurylochus.

ODYSSEUS

We're nearing the Sirens. Put wax in the men's ears.

Eurylochus hands out wax to the men. Odysseus looks ahead to the rocks, covered in light mist . . .

Eurylochus offers Odysseus the wax.

ODYSSEUS

No. Tie me to the mast.

EURYLOCHUS

Why?

ODYSSEUS

I want to hear the Sirens' song.

Eurylochus watches men TIE Odysseus to the mast . . .

EURYLOCHUS

This is a bad idea. No one's heard the song and lived.

Odysseus smiles at him –

ODYSSEUS

That's why it's a good idea – I'll be the first. No matter how I plead, do not untie me until we're well clear.

Eurylochus nods. Tests the knots. Steps back.

ODYSSEUS

Check the men's ears.

EURYLOCHUS

A WEEK'S RATIONS FOR THE FIRST 'YES, SIR!'

Nothing. The men keep working, oblivious. Odysseus nods, excited –

ODYSSEUS

Listen!

Eurylochus can hear the wind SINGING through the rigging . . .

Eurylochus reaches into the pot of beeswax, STOPPING up his ears – the sound becomes MUTED. Odysseus SHOUTS something, but we can't hear it at all, we hear only MUFFLED THUDS of oars and feet on deck . . . Eurylochus nods his head, marking time for the rowers visually . . .

Eurylochus looks at approaching rocks covered in light mist . . . above the breakers, SEALS lie on the rocks . . . Eurylochus spots PALER forms amongst the seals, barely visible in the mist. He stares, fascinated, trying to see if they are . . . human?

Glancing at the rowers, he sees them all STARING behind him –

He turns to Odysseus, then freezes, seeing Odysseus's expression . . . Odysseus is TRANSFIXED, his expression a combination of BLISS and TERROR . . .

EURYLOCHUS

(V.O.)

What was the Sirens' song?

ODYSSEUS

(V.O.)

All the things you'd want it to be. Then all things you wish you never wished for . . .

Odysseus STARES at the forms on the rocks, mouth OPEN in CRIES and CRIES, EXULTANT, FRUSTRATED . . .

A sailor, Anchialus, seeing Odysseus's reaction, PULLS the wax from his ear . . .

FLASH-FORWARD TO ODYSSEUS SITTING ON THE DECK RELAYING HIS EXPERIENCE –

ODYSSEUS

(V.O.)

It was the delicious itch you go to scratch . . .

Anchialus, in BLISSFUL MADNESS, STRUGGLES with his shipmates, breaking free – he DIVES off the side of the boat . . .

Eurylochus watches Odysseus STRUGGLE against the ropes – Odysseus looks at Eurylochus, PLEADING, CRYING, CRAZED . . .

ODYSSEUS
(V.O.)
But find it's under the skin, and can't be reached . . .

Eurylochus turns back to the men. He can't watch . . .

ODYSSEUS
(V.O.)
So the delicious itch becomes unbearable . . .

The ship glides past the rocks, passing close enough to make out NAKED FEMALE FORMS on the misty rocks, MOUTHS OPEN in song, sitting atop BONES and BONES . . .

ODYSSEUS
(V.O.)
It told you what you most want is what you most can't have, and what you most can't have is what you already had and lost . . .

Eurylochus turns back to Odysseus, who WEEPS BITTER TEARS . . .

Finally Odysseus SLUMPS against the ropes, passed out . . .

Eurylochus pulls the wax from his ears – once again we hear wind and water, the lapping of oars, the creaking of the deck.

ODYSSEUS
(V.O.)
It was the song of all the promises I've failed to keep . . .

Eurylochus gives Odysseus water as the men untie him from the mast. Odysseus looks up at Eurylochus. Haunted.

ODYSSEUS
And it told me I don't really want to go home.

Odysseus rubs tears of shame from his face. Eurylochus looks down at him. Pitying. The boat moves past the rocks into more open water . . .

A EXT. ODYSSEUS'S SHIP, CHARYBDIS – DAYA

A SHOUT from the lookout grabs Eurylochus's attention –

POLITES

White water!

He peers out to WHITECAPS on the horizon. An OMINOUS RUMBLE builds . . . Odysseus comes beside him . . .

EURYLOCHUS

Whitecaps? Out here?

ODYSSEUS

Charybdis.

EURYLOCHUS

What's that?

ODYSSEUS

A monstrous whirlpool.

Eurylochus jumps to the helm, looking out to the white water.

ODYSSEUS

Can we head out to sea?

The Helmsman, Antiphates, looks at the current pulling the ship –

ANTIPHATES

It's already got us . . .

Eurylochus looks to the cliffside . . . there is a narrow channel in a CANYON.

EURYLOCHUS

We might make that canyon . . .

Odysseus looks ahead to the mouth of the canyon, jagged rocks sticking out of the water across the mouth . . .

ODYSSEUS

It's too narrow.

He looks ahead to where the WHIRLPOOL has started to open up, the ocean DIPPING below the horizon in a DIZZYING sinkhole . . .

ODYSSEUS

Take us across the whirlpool.

EURYLOCHUS

Charybdis will suck us down and destroy us!

The ship is LEANING IN to the pull of the whirlpool . . . the channel entrance is coming up fast . . .

ODYSSEUS

Don't be afraid, we can make it! Steer down the slope, we can make enough way to shoot out the other side.

Eurylochus looks at the raging whirlpool, then at the channel mouth.

EURYLOCHUS

No!

(to Helmsman)

We're making for the channel!

Odysseus rushes for the tiller – two of the men GRAB him.

Odysseus lets himself be subdued as the ship SHOOTS into the channel mouth, over the RAPIDS, SKIMMING past SHEER ROCK WALLS . . .

The ship SCRAPES the side of the canyon, water BURSTING through split planks . . . men PUSH the boards back into place . . .

Odysseus looks up at the cliff faces, waiting for the inevitable. His men release him, the crew CHEERING as Eurylochus settles the ship in the channel past the rapids . . .

Eurylochus turns to Odysseus, TRIUMPHANT.

EURYLOCHUS

We made it.

Odysseus nods. Wary. At his oar, Polites turns to the man next to him . . .

POLITES

We did it. We –

POLITES IS RIPPED, SCREAMING from the ship by a TOOTH-FILLED set of jaws on a SNAKE NECK –

ANOTHER soldier is TAKEN – and ANOTHER . . .

SCREAMS ECHOING through the canyon . . . The Helmsman looks around, pulling the tiller –

ODYSSEUS

Keep her straight!

Odysseus SHOUTS at the men –

ODYSSEUS

PULL!

Three more men are RIPPED from the ship, SCREAMING, pulled up and into a DARK CREVICE of the cliff above . . .

SILENCE. Deafening silence. Everyone in shock. Eurylochus looks at Odysseus, DEVASTATED . . .

EURYLOCHUS

Why did I take us this way . . . ?

ODYSSEUS

It wasn't your fault.

EURYLOCHUS

What *was* that?

ODYSSEUS

Scylla.

Eurylochus looks back at the canyon, then to Odysseus . . .

EURYLOCHUS

Wait . . . you *knew*?

Odysseus says nothing.

EURYLOCHUS

You knew, and didn't tell us.

ODYSSEUS

If I'd told you, you wouldn't have chosen this way.

EURYLOCHUS

And those men would be alive!

ODYSSEUS

No. We'd all be dead.

EURYLOCHUS

You had no right.

ODYSSEUS

I had every right. And every responsibility. The whirlpool would've destroyed the ship and all of us. This way we live.

EURYLOCHUS

Some of us live.

ODYSSEUS

Yes. Some of us.

EURYLOCHUS

What else did Tiresias tell you?

Odysseus looks away. The crew glare at him. The ship emerges from the canyon.

EXT. ODYSSEUS'S SHIP, OFF APOLLO'S ISLAND – LATER

Eurylochus spots a low-lying island.

EURYLOCHUS

I'm going to put in there.

Odysseus, sitting, looks over at the island.

ODYSSEUS

That's the Sun God's isle. We can't land there.

The crew starts to COMPLAIN OPENLY.

EURYLOCHUS

We need repairs. These men are exhausted. They've lost six shipmates. We're going to put in and rest on dry land.

The men CHEER.

ODYSSEUS

You're all going to die.

They quiet, looking at Odysseus, who stands . . .

ODYSSEUS

You asked me what Tiresias told me. He said you're all going to die.

EURYLOCHUS

If we land on that island?

ODYSSEUS

If you slaughter the Sun God's cattle, which graze on that island, you'll all die.

EURYLOCHUS

That's fine. We'll put in and cook our own provisions. We'll pick fruit and get water. Nothing more.

Odysseus shakes his head, despairing. Looking at the desperation of his crew, the water leaking into the hull, he can see he has no choice but to agree . . .

ODYSSEUS

Swear to it. All of you. Swear you won't touch the cattle on this island.

The men nod at Odysseus. Eurylochus guides the ship in, GROUNDING the boat on the sand. There are COWS grazing just above the sand on the edge of the forest.

EURYLOCHUS

See, the wind took us right in. We'll rest up, do the repairs and set out as soon as the wind changes.

As the men jump off the ship, pointing and laughing at the cattle, Odysseus looks at the flag FLAPPING HARD at the onshore breeze, PERTURBED . . .

CALYPSO

(V.O.)

Did the crew keep their promise?

ODYSSEUS

(V.O.)

Yes. For a long time. But the wind never changed . . .

EXT. BEACH OUTSIDE CALYPSO'S CAVE – DAY

Odysseus rubs his hands across the bleached planks. Tenderly, as if they were the bones of an old friend . . .

ODYSSEUS

Day after day, week after week . . . The steady onshore breeze, which had made it so easy to land, made it impossible to leave . . .

EXT. BEACH, APOLLO'S ISLAND – DAY

The crew, thin and ragged, sit in the shade chewing on hard biscuit, casting looks at the FAT COWS wandering nearby . . .

ODYSSEUS
(V.O.)
And our provisions ran out.

EXT. ODYSSEUS'S SHIP – NIGHT

Odysseus stares up at the flag FLAPPING across the moon.

INSERT CUT: the STONE HEAD of Athena ROCKS from side to side in FLICKERING FIRELIGHT on DIRTY MARBLE . . .

Odysseus rises, staring into the forest. He can see FIRELIGHT deep in the trees . . . he sees Athena standing there, beckoning him towards the forest . . .

EXT. FOREST, APOLLO'S ISLAND – MOMENTS LATER

Odysseus makes his way through the trees, closing in on the flickering fire . . . Odysseus moves towards the fire, SMELLING something . . .

EXT. CLEARING, FOREST, APOLLO'S ISLAND – CONTINUOUS

Odysseus stands in the firelight, watching his crew SILENTLY FEAST. An OX, turns on a spit, fat bubbling deliciously.

One of the crew notices Odysseus standing in the shadows. One by one the men stop eating, looking at Odysseus, ashamed.

ODYSSEUS
Did you think if you ate quietly the Sun God wouldn't notice?

Eurylochus steps forward.

EURYLOCHUS
We thought *you* wouldn't notice.

ODYSSEUS
I'm not the problem . . .

Odysseus turns . . .

ODYSSEUS

I wanted you to live.

He melts back into the woods.

EXT. ODYSSEUS'S SHIP – MOMENTS LATER

Odysseus strides back to the ship. Athena falls in beside him . . .

ATHENA

Tiresias told you. Circe told you. The Gods told you –

ODYSSEUS

You Gods don't speak in ways we understand!

ATHENA

Who doesn't understand pain?! Or blood?! Or death?!

Odysseus shakes his head, hoping she won't be there any more. But Athena continues . . .

ATHENA

When you watch your men die do you see chance? Or do you see consequence?

Odysseus turns on her –

ODYSSEUS

I see consequence. I see my failure.

ATHENA

What if their deaths aren't your failing but theirs?

ODYSSEUS

I lead them. I led them here.

ATHENA

And who led you? Why do you put yourself above the Gods? Why do you claim responsibility? Why don't you want to go home?

Odysseus stares at her. Thinking. About to speak –

EURYLOCHUS
(O.S.)
What were they supposed to do?!

Odysseus turns to see Eurylochus approaching. Athena is gone.

EURYLOCHUS
(O.S.)
Our food ran out! Have some pity.

Odysseus turns, FURIOUS –

ODYSSEUS
My pity put us on this damned island! I told you what would happen.

EURYLOCHUS
Yes, you did. And we decided that we'd rather drown than starve.

Odysseus NOTICES – the flag has STOPPED FLAPPING. He POINTS at it –

ODYSSEUS
Well, here's our chance.

Eurylochus RUNS back towards the trees, SHOUTING.

The Crew push the boat off the sand, JUMPING aboard, PULLING on the oars, PUSHING out into the moonlight on the now-calm sea . . .

ODYSSEUS
(V.O.)
The calm was just long enough to tempt us out onto Poseidon's ocean. Under Zeus's sky . . .

EXT. ODYSSEUS'S SHIP – NIGHT

The ship PITCHES FRIGHTENINGLY down the back of a massive wave. The crew CLING to the oars as the ship is SMASHED by waves and wind. LIGHTNING FLASHES across a jagged, merciless sea. Odysseus HANGS ON to the rigging at the back of the ship.

Eurylochus tries to command the men – SCREAMING into the HOWLING WIND . . .

EURYLOCHUS

GET THE SAIL DOWN! GET THE OARS OUT! GATHER THE SAIL! TURN INTO THE WIND!

ODYSSEUS

EURYLOCHUS! GRAB SOMETHING! HANG ON!

Eurylochus is TOSSED like a rag doll as the ship BOTTOMS OUT at the foot of another wave – Odysseus WRAPS his arms around the mast, cheek pressed into the soaking wood . . . he hears it CRACKING inside . . . he JUMPS aside as the mast gives way, the GIANT WOODEN BEAM PLUNGING DOWN ONTO THE DECK – SMASHING EURYLOCHUS to the deck –

ODYSSEUS

EURYLOCHUS!

Odysseus CRAWLS on his belly to GRAB Eurylochus's hand . . . Eurylochus looks up at him, BLINKING, SEEKING HELP . . .

ODYSSEUS

(V.O.)

The last thing I remember was the harsh hand of Zeus . . .

A LIGHTNING BOLT DRILLS INTO THE SHIP, CRACKING IT IN HALF . . .

Odysseus SCREAMS as Eurylochus and the crew are YANKED away from him on a splintered section of ship . . .

INT. CALYPSO'S CAVE – NIGHT

Odysseus stares into his wine . . .

ODYSSEUS

I don't know what happened to my men.

CALYPSO

Yes, you do. Exactly what you told them would happen.

He looks at her. Nods gravely. Looks at his surroundings . . .

ODYSSEUS

I washed up on your shore alone.

CALYPSO

You washed up on my shore . . .

EXT. BEACH OUTSIDE CALYPSO'S CAVE – DAY (FLASHBACK)

Odysseus lies on the beach, surrounded by WRECKAGE.

CALYPSO

(V.O.)

With some of your boat. And none of your crew.

Calypso looks down on the ragged unconscious sailor, one fist clenched.

CALYPSO

(V.O.)

Half-dead. Unconscious.

INT. CALYPSO'S CAVE – NIGHT

Odysseus lies unconscious on a bed. Calypso uses a cloth to clean his arms and hands. His CLENCHED FIST *will not open for her . . .*

CALYPSO

(V.O.)

I watched you lost. For days. Into weeks.

Calypso crushes lotus flower in a mortar . . .

CALYPSO

(V.O.)

I knew the lotus would ease your awakening so your pain would be more of the body than the mind.

She gives him a drink to sip. His eyes, barely conscious, take her in.

CALYPSO
(V.O.)
And it did. You liked it so much, and ate it so happily . . .

Odysseus eats, hungrily. He smiles at Calypso . . .

CALYPSO
(V.O.)
And as I cared for you I came to love you.

INT. CALYPSO'S CAVE – NIGHT (PRESENT)

Odysseus stares at Calypso. Concerned.

ODYSSEUS
How long have I been here?

CALYPSO
I kept telling myself to stop giving it to you. That you were strong enough to remember . . .

ODYSSEUS
How long, Calypso?

CALYPSO
But you were so happy.

ODYSSEUS
You were happy.

CALYPSO
We were happy. For years.

ODYSSEUS
Years?!

CALYPSO
Seven years.

Odysseus takes this in. He looks at her, quiet . . .

ODYSSEUS

You fed me lotus flower and held me captive –

CALYPSO

I saved your life.

Odysseus shakes his head. Lost . . .

CALYPSO

I rebuilt your body. But I couldn't bring myself to rebuild your mind. And you've been happy. But your heart was always elsewhere, your mind was bound to follow eventually.

ODYSSEUS

How could you?

CALYPSO

The lotus clouds the mind and saps the will – but it doesn't change who you are. You weren't ready to go home, for whatever reason.

ODYSSEUS

I am now.

CALYPSO

As I always knew you would be.

ODYSSEUS

How?

CALYPSO

You were clutching something when I found you. Your hand didn't open for weeks . . .

She holds out the golden pin of Athena given to him by Penelope . . .

CALYPSO

You used to call out in your sleep. Mostly to Athena, but sometimes you'd say another name . . .

Odysseus takes the golden pin, turns it in his fingers – remembers with a JOLT –

ODYSSEUS

Penelope.

Calypso nods. Odysseus REELS with the flood of memories . . .

ODYSSEUS

Help me go home.

CALYPSO

I am.

EXT. BEACH OUTSIDE CALYPSO'S CAVE – DAY

Odysseus STRAPS the planks of his CRUDE RAFT together.

CALYPSO

(V.O.)

You're a man who needs to control his fate, but you cannot control this . . .

He pulls it down to the shore . . .

CALYPSO

(V.O.)

You must give yourself to the storm, give yourself to Poseidon, take your punishment . . .

Pushes it out onto the waves . . . Calypso watches . . .

CALYPSO

(V.O.)

Zeus won't let him kill you . . .

EXT. RAFT – DAY

Odysseus lies back on the raft, staring at the sky, riding the swell . . . DRIFTING . . . as the sea RISES . . .

CALYPSO

(V.O.)

Give up the fight. Give up control. And live. It's a leap of faith you've never yet made, Odysseus.

Close on Odysseus as he CLINGS to the raft, WATER STREAMING ACROSS HIM. ENDLESSLY . . . DROWNING . . . CLEARLY DROWNING . . .

INSERT CUT: a BRONZE SWORD DECAPITATES a STONE STATUE OF ATHENA, SPARKING, the head TUMBLING in FLICKERING FIRELIGHT. It comes to rest on FILTHY MARBLE, ROCKING from side to side as if SHAKING HER HEAD . . .

EXT. FOGGY BEACH – DAWN

Odysseus lies on his back, staring up at the sky . . .

FEMALE VOICE
(O.S.)

Odysseus?

Odysseus raises his head. Athena is sitting further up the sand.

ODYSSEUS

Where am I?

Athena smiles at him.

ATHENA

Don't you recognize your own home?

Odysseus looks around. Dazed.

ODYSSEUS

Ithaca?

Athena is gone. Odysseus. Old, grey-bearded, ragged, weathered, stumbles up the shore of his beloved Ithaca. Home at last.

EXT. CLIFFS OF ITHACA – DAY

Eumaeus is tending the pigs with his dogs. One of them starts BARKING. Eumaeus follows the barking dog to the fence.

EUMAEUS

Who's there?

It is Irus. With a group of BANDITS . . .

IRUS

We need food.

Several young FARMHANDS have gathered behind Eumaeus to quiet the dogs. Eumaeus's words are friendly, but the tone shows CLEAR DISTRUST.

EUMAEUS

Zeus welcomes you, strangers. How many are you?

Irus leans on the gate . . . quietly opening it . . .

IRUS

A dozen.

The Bandits quietly come through the fence to surround Eumaeus. The dogs BARK. Eumaeus SHUSHES them, sternly.

EUMAEUS

In need of a meal?

IRUS

And supplies. For the road.

EUMAEUS

Where are you headed?

IRUS

We need pigs – we're going all the way to Pylos.

EUMAEUS

Are you pilgrims?

Several Bandits LAUGH.

IRUS

Do we look like pilgrims?

EUMAEUS

I don't see well. Zeus demands I offer you a meal, but these pigs aren't mine to sell.

IRUS

Don't worry, we're not paying . . .

Irus nods at his men who DRAW BRONZE with a distinctive SCRAPE . . . the dogs BARK . . . the Farmhands RUN, SCREAMING . . .

Eumaeus swings his stick blindly . . .

INT. PALACE OF MENELAUS – DAY

Telemachus and Mentor approach the throne. Menelaus and Helen sit, waiting to receive them.

TELEMACHUS

Thank you for your hospitality. And your advice.

HELEN

Are you sure you have to leave us?

Telemachus looks at Menelaus.

TELEMACHUS

I'm sure. I should be at home.

HELEN

Give my greetings to your mother.

MENELAUS

I'm sorry I had no news of your father.

TELEMACHUS

You had news. Not where he is, but who he is. And now more than ever . . .

EXT. CLIFFS OF ITHACA – EVENING

Odysseus, hooded and cloaked as a beggar, walks up the road, tasting the air of home, contented. Heading towards some PLUMES OF SMOKE.

TELEMACHUS

(V.O.)

I hope to meet him one day.

Recognizing, in the distance, his pig farm, he smiles . . .

As he comes closer he sees Eumaeus, with a young Farmhand, tending to one of several LARGE BONFIRES. Odysseus smiles at the sight of his old friend. As he approaches he calls out –

ODYSSEUS
Where are your watchdogs, old man?!

Eumaeus, BRUISED and BLOODY, turns tearful, sightless eyes towards Odysseus . . .

EUMAEUS
I'm burning their bodies.

Odysseus's smile falls. The battered old man gathers his dignity . . .

EUMAEUS
Can Zeus offer you food and drink, stranger?

Eumaeus sends off his Farmhand. Odysseus looks, appalled. Eumaeus is on the verge of collapse . . .

ODYSSEUS
Were you attacked?

Eumaeus nods. Odysseus watches the young Farmhand walking to the farmhouse . . .

ODYSSEUS
The dogs saved your farmhands.

Eumaeus shakes his head . . .

EUMAEUS
We burned his brothers first.

Odysseus looks at the other fires with suppressed rage.

ODYSSEUS
What's happened to Ithaca?

EUMAEUS
Darkness. Zeus's law smashed to pieces. A kingdom without a king since my master died.

ODYSSEUS

Who was your master?

EUMAEUS

Odysseus.

ODYSSEUS

Odysseus? Hero of the Trojan War? He's not dead –

EUMAEUS

DON'T!!

Eumaeus TURNS on Odysseus, FLAILING BLINDLY at him –

EUMAEUS

BEGGARS GIVING FALSE HOPE! NO MORE! NO MORE!

Odysseus gently holds Eumaeus's arms, embracing him as he COLLAPSES – Odysseus calls out to the farmhand to help . . .

INT. EUMAEUS'S FARMHOUSE – NIGHT

Odysseus tends to Eumaeus who is laid out on his cot. The Farmhand brings water . . . Eumaeus is weeping . . .

EUMAEUS

Telemachus. If I weren't blind, I could help Telemachus –

ODYSSEUS

Telemachus?

EUMAEUS

He's in danger. I can't help him.

ODYSSEUS

There must be others in Ithaca who'd help Odysseus's son.

EUMAEUS

The palace is controlled by suitors. No one's still loyal to Odysseus.

Odysseus doesn't want to ask . . .

ODYSSEUS

What about the Queen?

Eumaeus smiles, fondly.

EUMAEUS

Beautiful, wise Penelope. Held hostage by the worst men. Soon to be forced into marriage. What can she do without even her son?

ODYSSEUS

What's the danger to Telemachus?

EUMAEUS

He's on his way back from Sparta. The suitors sent bandits to Pylos to ambush him at the temple.

Odysseus RISES, turns to the Farmhand –

ODYSSEUS

Give me food for the road.

EUMAEUS

You'll never catch up with the bandits.

ODYSSEUS

If I'm at Pylos when Telemachus arrives, I can warn him.

The Farmhand wraps a bundle for Odysseus.

EUMAEUS

Why are you helping?

Odysseus takes the bundle. Turns to Eumaeus on the bed . . .

ODYSSEUS

If I tell you, don't be angry.

Eumaeus nods.

ODYSSEUS

I served under Odysseus at Troy.

Eumaeus takes this in. Suppressing his usual instincts.

EUMAEUS

Really?

ODYSSEUS

Yes. He was a harsh taskmaster.

EUMAEUS

But fair. And worthy of following.

Odysseus looks at the blind old man. Welling up.

ODYSSEUS

You loved him.

EUMAEUS

Like a son.

Odysseus moves to the door. Needs to say more . . .

ODYSSEUS

Well, he is not dead.

Eumaeus takes this in. Allowing himself to believe . . .

EUMAEUS

Is he coming home?

ODYSSEUS

Soon.

EUMAEUS

Bringing vengeance?

ODYSSEUS

Bringing it all.

Odysseus leaves Eumaeus with a painful sense of hope.

EXT. SHIP OFF COAST OF ITHACA AT PYLOS – DUSK

Telemachus stares at the flickering fires on the cliffs. Mentor speaks to the PILOT as they dock.

MENTOR

Head down the coast to the harbour. The suitors may be waiting there. You've come from Crete on a trading mission.

PILOT

We don't have a cargo.

MENTOR

Seized by pirates.

The Pilot nods. A party of six SOLDIERS assembles behind Telemachus.

EXT. CAVE TEMPLE AT PYLOS – MOMENTS LATER

Telemachus's party makes its way towards large OPENINGS in the cliffs . . .

MENTOR

I'll talk. We don't want anyone realizing who you are.

TELEMACHUS

Maybe we shouldn't have brought a guard.

MENTOR

We'll be glad we did if there's trouble on the road.

EXT. CAVE TEMPLE, PYLOS – NIGHT

Mentor, Telemachus and their men make their way through the encampments to the steps of the temple . . . passing through a mass of seated Pilgrims and BEGGARS WHO RISE TO APPROACH, hands outstretched. The Guard PUSHES them away from Telemachus.

BEGGAR

Hey! I have a message!

A Guard brutally PUSHES the Beggar down – as he lands we see IT IS ODYSSEUS.

ODYSSEUS

Wait!

The party arrives at the top of the stairs, met by PRIESTS . . .

ODYSSEUS

Eumaeus sent me!

Telemachus TURNS at the sound of Eumaeus's name, but is shepherded into the temple by the Priests . . .

INT. TEMPLE, PYLOS – CONTINUOUS

Telemachus, Mentor and the party are escorted through the PILGRIMS by a PRIEST. Telemachus turns to Mentor –

TELEMACHUS

Bring that beggar – he has a message from Eumaeus.

Mentor sends one of the Guard. The Priest leads them down through the tunnels of the dark temple. Telemachus spots various groups of WORSHIPPERS in FIRELIT ALCOVES as they move deeper and deeper . . . Down into a dark sanctuary . . .

PRIEST

Your men must stay out here.

Mentor nods at his men, who FORM UP around the opening.

PRIEST

Your weapons, too.

Telemachus and Mentor remove their swords and daggers, handing them to the nearest of their Guard . . .

INT. INNER SANCTUM, TEMPLE, PYLOS – CONTINUOUS

Telemachus and Mentor enter the CALM of the inner sanctum. A statue of Athena is lit from below by votive offerings. They are greeted by six PRIESTS. The HEAD PRIEST steps forward . . . IT IS IRUS, in disguise . . .

IRUS

Zeus welcomes you, strangers.

Cleaner, and wearing the robes of a priest, his edge is still apparent to Telemachus.

TELEMACHUS

Thank you.

Irus motions a Priest to hand Telemachus and Mentor cups of wine.

IRUS

Have you travelled far?

Telemachus sniffs the wine, but caution stops him drinking. Mentor GULPS his down . . .

TELEMACHUS

Not that far.

IRUS

You're here to rest for the night?

Mentor frowns at Irus, confused . . .

TELEMACHUS

We're here to make sacrifice to Athena. Then whatever hospitality you can offer might be considered.

IRUS

Of course.

Telemachus notices a SPOT OF BLOOD on the Irus's sleeve . . . Odysseus is PUSHED inside the room.

IRUS

Get this beggar out of here.

Telemachus looks around at Odysseus in his rags.

TELEMACHUS

He has a message for me.

Irus looks at Odysseus, challenging.

TELEMACHUS

Eumaeus sent you?

ODYSSEUS MARVELS AT HIS GROWN-UP SON . . .

ODYSSEUS

Yes, sir.

TELEMACHUS

What's the message?

Odysseus looks at Irus. And the other Priests.

ODYSSEUS

It's private.

TELEMACHUS

These men are Priests . . .

Odysseus says nothing . . . the SILENCE STRETCHES . . .

Mentor CHOKES, DROPPING to his knees – Odysseus REACHES down, GRABBING him. Mentor, IN AGONY, looks into Odysseus's eyes . . . RECOGNIZES HIM . . . just as he dies.

The Priests DRAW DAGGERS –

Odysseus, head down, RISES between them and Telemachus.

IRUS

This is your moment to leave, old man.

TELEMACHUS

Go, stranger.

Odysseus slowly shakes his lowered head . . .

IRUS

I spared one old man this week, but he was blind. I won't spare another.

Two Priests BAR THE DOOR – a Priest moves towards Odysseus, blade held out – Odysseus JAMS the Priest's own knife into his throat – the Priest DROPS. Everyone STARES at Odysseus . . .

Irus LUNGES, Odysseus GRABS his arm and STABS the Priest next to him – a Priest LUNGES at Telemachus, who SMASHES his cup into the Priest's face – Telemachus DUCKS, ROLLS, COMING UP to grab a Priest, SMASHING him into the bars of the screen –

INT. TEMPLE, PYLOS – CONTINUOUS

Outside the inner sanctum, the Guards are ATTACKED by Priests –

INT. INNER SANCTUM, TEMPLE, PYLOS – CONTINUOUS

Odysseus GRABS a Priest from behind, SEIZES his dagger.

Telemachus SPINS – three Priests in front of him, all armed . . .

ODYSSEUS

Here!

Odysseus TOSSES him a dagger – then PILES into the nearest Priest, making BRUTAL HAVOC – Telemachus STABS the nearest Priest, then turns to see Odysseus POUND the remaining Priests into the floor of Athena's temple . . . Telemachus looks at him, IMPRESSED.

Odysseus finishes, rises. Breathing hard.

TELEMACHUS

Pretty good for a beggar.

ODYSSEUS

(breathless)

I wasn't born a beggar.

Odysseus pulls a robe off one of the dead priests. Telemachus checks Mentor's body. Odysseus turns – sees Telemachus grieving Mentor.

ODYSSEUS

Put on that priest's robes.

TELEMACHUS

We need help with the body.

Odysseus tosses Telemachus the priest's robes.

ODYSSEUS

We have to leave him.

TELEMACHUS

No.

ODYSSEUS

We have to slip out –

TELEMACHUS

This isn't how you honour the dead –

ODYSSEUS

It's how you stay alive.

TELEMACHUS

He was my teacher. He may have been Athena in disguise. I'm not leaving him.

Odysseus looks at Telemachus, sympathetic.

ODYSSEUS

His name is Mentor. And when you're safe we'll head into the unknown west and honour him.

(gestures at dead priests)

These men were sent by the suitors. There'll be more, we have to get on the road.

TELEMACHUS

By night?

ODYSSEUS

Safer than staying here.

He pours the oil from the lamp on the floor –

ODYSSEUS

Mentor's at the heart of Athena's oldest temple – for now, honour him in flame.

Telemachus reluctantly takes the lamp, looking down at Mentor's body. And drops it, SPREADING FLAME . . .

INT. TEMPLE, PYLOS – MOMENTS LATER

Chaos. Odysseus and Telemachus move up through the FLAMING TEMPLE.

Surrounded by PANICKING PILGRIMS, some RUSHING in with water to douse the flames . . .

EXT. CAVE TEMPLE, PYLOS – CONTINUOUS

They make their way out of the temple and into the encampments . . .

EXT. ROAD, ITHACA – DAWN

Telemachus and Odysseus walk side by side in silence.

TELEMACHUS
How does a beggar come to know Mentor?

ODYSSEUS
I told you, I wasn't always a beggar.

TELEMACHUS
You have wise eyes. Athena's eyes –

ODYSSEUS
Don't look for Gods in men – you'll always be disappointed.

Telemachus stops. Takes Odysseus by the arm. Aggressive.

TELEMACHUS
Then tell me who you are.

Odysseus looks at Telemachus. Starts walking again.

ODYSSEUS

My name is Sinon. I'm an old soldier who fought under your father at Troy.

TELEMACHUS

You knew my father?

ODYSSEUS

I've taken his orders longer than I care to remember.

Telemachus notices the tense –

TELEMACHUS

He's alive?!

Odysseus takes a few paces to form his answer . . .

ODYSSEUS

He's alive.

TELEMACHUS

Where is he?

ODYSSEUS

Close by. He sent me ahead to assess the situation.

TELEMACHUS

My mother won't believe it –

ODYSSEUS

You can't tell her.

TELEMACHUS

Nothing?

ODYSSEUS

Tell her you've decided it's time she remarried.

Telemachus realizes.

TELEMACHUS

He doesn't need to test my mother. How can he doubt her?

ODYSSEUS

He doesn't. But she has every reason to have forgotten him. Are there any loyal servants?

TELEMACHUS

Some. When Odysseus shows himself? All.

ODYSSEUS

We need to gather the suitors in the palace.

TELEMACHUS

Never a problem.

Odysseus looks him up and down . . .

ODYSSEUS

Do you have gifts from Menelaus?

TELEMACHUS

On my ship.

ODYSSEUS

Good. Come back as a prince. Call a banquet. I'll be there.

TELEMACHUS

What will you do at the banquet?

ODYSSEUS

Beg. The clearest view of a person is from below. How many suitors are there?

TELEMACHUS

Dozens. But if all his men are like you –

ODYSSEUS

He has no men. He's coming back, but he has no men.

TELEMACHUS

Just you?

Odysseus looks at Telemachus and smiles.

ODYSSEUS

And you.

INT. EUMAEUS'S HUT – DAY

Eumaeus is preparing food . . .

ODYSSEUS
(O.S.)
Glad to see you on your feet.

Eumaeus turns to the sound of his voice. Odysseus is rifling through a pile of LEATHER STRAPS . . .

ODYSSEUS
Because it's about time we took you back to the palace.

Eumaeus smiles.

EXT. TOWN, ITHACA – DAY

Telemachus walks, ALONE, dressed as a prince, through the town. The TOWNSPEOPLE start to notice. Running ahead with the news . . .

EXT. PALACE AT ITHACA – DAY

As Telemachus climbs the steps the GATEKEEPERS recognize him. A SHOUT goes up . . .

INT. MEGARON – MOMENTS LATER

Antinous PULLS Melantho into the shadows, embracing her . . .

MELANTHO
They're saying Telemachus is back –

ANTINOUS
What?

He looks at her –

ANTINOUS
Who is?

Penelope BURSTS from behind the screen –

PENELOPE
Where's Telemachus?!

Melantho separates from Antinous, hurrying over to Penelope, gesturing at the screen –

MELANTHO

My Queen, surely your place is up there?

Penelope glances at Melantho, sees Antinous . . .

Telemachus walks into the hall, trailed by servants pulling off his magnificent armour . . .

PENELOPE

It's true! You're home!

TELEMACHUS

I'm back.

Penelope EMBRACES her son . . .

TELEMACHUS

I thought we'd celebrate tonight . . .

Telemachus looks at Antinous.

TELEMACHUS

If we've got anything left to celebrate with.

PENELOPE

Don't worry, my brave suitors will shower us with gifts in honour of your return . . .

Penelope turns to Antinous. Who looks warmly at Telemachus.

ANTINOUS

I'm glad to see you've returned safely.

INT. PENELOPE'S CHAMBER, PALACE OF ITHACA – MOMENTS LATER

Melantho hands Telemachus a drink. Penelope waves her off.

TELEMACHUS

Menelaus –

Penelope gestures SILENCE. Waits for Melantho to leave . . .

PENELOPE

What did you hear about your father?

TELEMACHUS

Nothing. Stories from the war. But no one knew what happened to him after he left Troy. I'm sorry, Mom.

Penelope hides her disappointment. Telemachus looks away.

TELEMACHUS

Everybody in Sparta's talking about a coming catastrophe, an age of darkness brought on by people from the sea violating Zeus's law.

PENELOPE

So the stories are true. Our civilization *is* collapsing.

TELEMACHUS

Menelaus is concerned that we can't raise an army with an empty throne. We came up with a plan.

Penelope looks at him, surprised.

PENELOPE

What plan?

TELEMACHUS

The one way to get these suitors to leave. It's time for you to choose.

Penelope looks at him, SHOCKED.

PENELOPE

You want me to remarry?

TELEMACHUS

If you remarry, the other suitors will leave. I'm almost of age, I'll tell the Elders I learned of Odysseus's death in Sparta. Menelaus will back me up. They'll let me assume the throne.

PENELOPE

So you deny your father and I leave my home to go live with one of these snakes? That's your plan?!

TELEMACHUS

You have a better one?

PENELOPE

Lock the door, set a fire and burn the bastards.

Penelope squares up to her son, looking into his eyes –

PENELOPE

Telemachus, you think if I remarry life goes back to the way it was? That world is gone, and in *this* one they're not giving up power to you. Or Odysseus. If he returned he'd have to kill them. Like you will.

TELEMACHUS

If I kill the Suitors their families will demand revenge – I'll be exiled. And without me the throne will be lost.

PENELOPE

Because only a man can sit on it. 'Empty throne' – I've been sitting on that empty throne for twenty years. My knowledge, my years of experience – that's all nothing compared with the bristles on your chin.

She turns her back on him. He looks down at his feet, ashamed.

TELEMACHUS

Do you want peace, or do you want revenge?

PENELOPE

I want Odysseus.

BANG!

BARD

(*V.O.*)

Sing, muse, of a face.

INT. MEGARON, PALACE OF ITHACA – NIGHT

BANG! The Bard beats his rhythm atop the table . . .

BARD

A face.

BANG! Telemachus walks the room, watching the Suitors STREAM IN to the feast . . .

BARD

A fleet.

BANG!

EXT. TOWN, ITHACA – CONTINUOUS

Odysseus and Eumaeus make their way through the town.

Odysseus's hungry eyes eat up every sight in the town he hasn't seen for twenty years. He sees the palace . . .

BARD
(V.O.)

A war.

BANG!

INT. MEGARON, PALACE OF ITHACA – CONTINUOUS

The gathering Suitors stare up at the Bard. All except Antinous, who watches Telemachus head outside . . .

BARD

At Troy.

BANG!

BARD

Sing, muse, of a man.

BANG!

EXT. COURTYARD, PALACE OF ITHACA – CONTINUOUS

Telemachus watches Odysseus and Eumaeus climb the stairs to the palace.

BARD
(O.S.)

A man.

BANG!

Odysseus lets Eumaeus go ahead as he takes in his old home, TEARS welling, MEMORIES tumbling in . . .

BARD
(O.S.)

A thought.

BANG!

Telemachus sees Argus lying on the dung pile . . . Odysseus shuffles towards him like the old beggar he is dressed as . . .

BARD
(O.S.)

A trick.

Telemachus sees Odysseus notice Argus . . . thinks . . .

BANG!

Odysseus stares at the ancient dog lying on the dung pile as if dead . . .

ODYSSEUS

Eumaeus, go ahead.

At the sound of Odysseus's voice, Argus's EYES OPEN. Odysseus crouches to rub the dog's threadbare grey fur . . .

ODYSSEUS
(quiet)

Argus . . .

Argus's tail gives a WEAK WAG . . .

ODYSSEUS

Argus . . .

Now ARGUS IS DEAD. Odysseus nods at his old friend, ONE LAST PAT, then straightens . . . to find Telemachus, right there –

ODYSSEUS
You should bury him up on the cliffs.

TELEMACHUS
Where you met.

Odysseus just looks at his son, tears in his eyes.

TELEMACHUS
(quiet)
You're Odysseus. You're my father.

ODYSSEUS
I'm a beggar, and you . . . you're the worthy, beautiful son of Odysseus, of whom, when you do finally meet, he will be so proud . . .

Telemachus looks into his father's eyes . . .

TELEMACHUS
(louder)
Welcome, stranger.

Telemachus turns inside, CALLING over his shoulder –

INT. MEGARON, PALACE OF ITHACA – CONTINUOUS

TELEMACHUS
Accept the hospitality of Zeus.

Antinous looks up to see Telemachus indicate a place on the threshold for Odysseus to sit amongst other beggars, then hail a servant –

TELEMACHUS
Get the stranger some food.

ODYSSEUS
No, sir. Just let me make the rounds with my bowl.

Telemachus SHRUGS. Heads to his table –

Antinous steps in his path, speaking quietly.

ANTINOUS

You don't have enough guests, so you have to invite some filthy old plate licker to dinner?

Telemachus looks at Antinous. Shakes his head.

TELEMACHUS

What's one more beggar at this feast?

Telemachus confidently BRUSHES past Antinous. Antinous, SURPRISED, watches Telemachus move to his table with Eumaeus. Antinous moves to Polybus, as the Bard is replaced by DANCERS . . .

Odysseus, sitting on the threshold, looks up to where he can see Penelope's SILHOUETTE behind the screen.

He stares at the flicker from the oil lamps that reveal her . . .

Antinous, sitting by Polybus, leans in, speaking without looking.

ANTINOUS

We have to kill him before he regains his position and goes to the Elders.

Odysseus RISES to make the rounds with his begging bowl . . .

POLYBUS

How?

Telemachus watches the Suitors react to Odysseus. Most give him bread, some meat, some ignore him.

ANTINOUS

We provoke him to grab one of those weapons –

He indicates the weapons on the walls. Polybus looks at Telemachus presiding over the feast . . .

POLYBUS

He's not the same young pup we used to bait . . .

Antinous looks at Polybus. Hard.

ANTINOUS

Then we come back tonight and cut his throat.

Odysseus SHAKES his begging bowl at Polybus.

POLYBUS

Fuck off, old man.

ODYSSEUS

Please. It's days since I've eaten.

POLYBUS

I told you –

ODYSSEUS

You can't be generous with food that's not even yours?

Several of the Suitors LAUGH at this.

POLYBUS

There's no room in your bowl.

ODYSSEUS

Yes, there is.

Polybus takes the rim of the bowl, FLIPS it over, spilling the food onto the floor. Flipping it back, he looks into the empty bowl.

POLYBUS

So there is.

He pulls some of the bread he's chewing out of his mouth and puts it into the bowl.

POLYBUS

There you go.

As the other suitors LAUGH, Odysseus patiently CROUCHES DOWN to put each piece of the spilled food back into his bowl. Antinous looks at Telemachus, sees his BARELY SUPPRESSED RAGE . . .

Just as Odysseus's fingertips touch the last piece of bread, Antinous STEPS on it. Odysseus stops. Sighs.

ANTINOUS

Sorry, go ahead.

He lifts his foot off the crushed, filthy bread.

ANTINOUS

I suppose you want something from me now?

Odysseus gets to his feet, hunched over. Humble.

ODYSSEUS

No. I have something for you.

Antinous LAUGHS –

ANTINOUS

You have something for *me*?

The other Suitors laugh at this . . .

ANTINOUS

What could a filthy old plate licker like you possibly have that I could want?

Odysseus FUMBLES in his rags.

ODYSSEUS

Actually, it's yours –

He DROPS something into Antinous's bowl. It is the LOT.

ODYSSEUS

I was asked to return it.

Antinous STARES at it. The NOTCHES on its side . . .

ANTINOUS

That's not mine.

ODYSSEUS

No?

Antinous picks up the lot, staring at it.

ANTINOUS

Where did you get this?

Odysseus walks away.

ANTINOUS

Don't turn your back on me!

Odysseus keeps walking – Antinous picks up a STOOL – HURLS it at Odysseus, HITTING him HARD on the shoulder. Odysseus STUMBLES, but doesn't go down. EVERYTHING STOPS, GOES QUIET . . . Odysseus stands there, doing nothing.

AMPHIMEDON

Antinous, you can't treat a beggar like that.

ELATUS

Zeus's law . . .

Antinous turns to the assembled –

ANTINOUS

Zeus's law?! You think this is a God in disguise?!

He turns to Odysseus who is still frozen –

ANTINOUS

Are you?! Are you a God in disguise, plate licker?!

ODYSSEUS

No. I'm a veteran of the Trojan War.

ANTINOUS

What's your name?

ODYSSEUS

Sinon.

Antinous FLINCHES, GLANCING into his bowl at the lot . . .

ODYSSEUS

Does that name mean something to you?

ANTINOUS

No.

ODYSSEUS

I use it to honour the bravest young man I ever met.

POLYBUS

Wasn't that your shepherd's son?

ANTINOUS

I don't remember –

POLYBUS

He wanted you to take his place.

Antinous picks up the lot, moves to Odysseus, grabbing him by the shoulder, SPINNING him around –

ANTINOUS

Where did you get this?!

Odysseus, head down, leans in, speaking softly . . .

ODYSSEUS

Where you'll soon be.

ANTINOUS

Where's that?

ODYSSEUS

Hades.

Antinous KICKS Odysseus to the ground –

TELEMACHUS

(O.S.)

ENOUGH!

Antinous and the other Suitors turn to Telemachus, SHOCKED.

TELEMACHUS

The feast is done.

All are surprised by the AUTHORITY of his tone.

The Suitors start to rise and file out . . .

The silhouette of Penelope talks to Melantho, who emerges from the screen, heading towards Odysseus, who sits to one side, curled up, avoiding the departing Suitors . . .

Antinous is standing, enraged, staring at the lot in his hand. Polybus pulls on his arm.

POLYBUS

Let's go. Antinous. Come on.

Antinous follows Polybus out, TOSSING the lot at Odysseus . . .

ANTINOUS

This is *not* mine.

Melantho bends down to Odysseus.

MELANTHO

The Queen would like to speak with you.

Odysseus looks at Penelope's silhouette.

MELANTHO

Stay here until everyone's left and the fires are lit.

Odysseus nods, looking down at his old, filthy hands. Then back to the silhouette . . .

INT. MEGARON, PALACE OF ITHACA – LATER

The megaron is quiet and empty. The feast has been cleared. Eumaeus tends the fires. Odysseus sits in the shadows, waiting . . .

Melantho waves him over. Telemachus watches his father shuffle across the great hall to climb the steps to Penelope's silhouette . . .

Odysseus sits on the steps by the screen. Penelope is right there, on the other side.

PENELOPE

Hello, traveller.

ODYSSEUS

My Queen.

PENELOPE

Melantho, have Eurycleia wash this stranger's feet.

ODYSSEUS

That's not necessary –

PENELOPE

My husband insisted we honour guests as family. You know of Odysseus, my husband?

ODYSSEUS

Of course.

PENELOPE

From the songs?

ODYSSEUS

I was at Troy, ma'am.

PENELOPE

Then the songs probably seem silly.

ODYSSEUS

They make me cry.

On the other side of the screen, Penelope leans closer.

PENELOPE

Why?

ODYSSEUS

For what was lost.

PENELOPE

The lives?

ODYSSEUS

And the years. Everything.

Penelope nods at this. Her voice is barely a whisper . . .

PENELOPE

Did you know Odysseus at Troy?

ODYSSEUS

I did.

Eurycleia arrives with a bowl – she is THE OLD NURSEMAID . . . Odysseus WATCHES her place the bowl at his feet . . .

Penelope leans towards the screen, breathlessly hopeful . . .

PENELOPE

Was there some detail of how he dressed . . . something he wore?

ODYSSEUS

He wore a strange brooch.

PENELOPE

Strange?

Odysseus smiles to himself . . .

ODYSSEUS

Beautiful. But out of place . . .

PENELOPE

Describe it.

The Old Nursemaid moves to wash Odysseus's feet – FREEZES, SEEING THE SCAR ON HIS ANKLE given to him by the WILD BOAR – she GASPS – LOOKS UP –

OLD NURSEMAID

Sir?!

Odysseus KICKS the bowl, tipping the water out.

ODYSSEUS

Sorry.

ACROSS THE HALL: the CLATTERING BOWL attracts the attention of Antinous and Polybus, who have returned. They step back into the shadows as Telemachus, at the fire, looks up to see HIS PARENTS, so close but so far apart . . .

Odysseus has his hand on the Old Nursemaid's chin, looking at her – she looks back, AMAZED – Odysseus SLIGHTLY SHAKES his head, warning her . . . she NODS, collects the bowl, SMILING to herself, EXCITED –

OLD NURSEMAID

I'll get more water.

Odysseus turns back to the screen. He can hear Penelope breathing on the other side . . .

ODYSSEUS

It was a beautiful gold pin. A figure of Athena, encircled by vines.

Penelope closes her eyes.

PENELOPE

Did he wear it often?

ODYSSEUS

He never took it off.

She starts to weep . . .

DEEP IN THE SHADOWS, Antinous pulls his dagger, checking the blade. He lies it across his lap, settling in, watching Telemachus stare at his parents . . .

Odysseus leans slightly towards the screen.

PENELOPE

How did you make it home, when Odysseus could not?

ODYSSEUS

I'm not home. Not yet.

PENELOPE

Why not?

ODYSSEUS

It's not always an easy thing, a homecoming. That's as true for Odysseus as for me.

PENELOPE

The Odysseus I knew would've found or fought his way back to me no matter what.

ODYSSEUS

What if the Odysseus you knew lost his way?

Odysseus looks to one side. Athena is there, sitting next to him . . . she gently shakes her head at him . . .

ODYSSEUS

What if, one night in a strange city, he saw things that made him think the home he knew couldn't possibly be there any more?

Odysseus closes his eyes . . .

EXT. TROY – NIGHT (FLASHBACK)

The great Wooden Horse stands in the moonlight before the Temple of Athena . . . Odysseus CLIMBS down from the belly . . .

ODYSSEUS

(V.O.)

What if when he left the belly of the Horse . . .

EXT. GATES OF TROY – NIGHT (FLASHBACK)

Odysseus signals the TORCHES to DROP. The gates to be opened . . .

ODYSSEUS

(V.O.)

. . . And opened the gates of Troy . . .

The VAST GATES open. AGAMEMNON stands there in the moonlight. RIVERS OF GREEK WARRIORS stream past him on either side . . .

ODYSSEUS

(V.O.)

He saw ten years of rage pour into that city in one night . . .

THOUSANDS of Greek Warriors race through the streets, SETTING FIRES, pulling people from houses and MURDERING them in the streets . . . the TROJAN WARRIORS race into the streets, still PUTTING ON THEIR ARMOUR, they are CUT DOWN by the MURDEROUS GREEKS FLYING through the narrow streets . . . Odysseus CLASHES BRONZE with Trojans as he races back up towards the temple . . . he RACES into the square, STOPS, TURNING AROUND IN PLACE TO WITNESS CARNAGE ALL AROUND . . .

A Trojan is UPON Odysseus, HACKING at him, FURIOUSLY . . . Eurylochus STABS the Trojan, SAVING Odysseus . . . Eurylochus offers his hand, pulling Odysseus to his feet – they run under the Horse towards the temple . . .

INT. MEGARON, PALACE OF ITHACA – NIGHT (BACK TO PRESENT)

Odysseus still has his eyes closed . . .

ODYSSEUS

We left them a *gift*. An offering of *peace* that they took into their *home*.

Odysseus opens his eyes to look at Athena, who is CRYING. On the other side of the screen, Penelope listens, appalled . . .

ODYSSEUS

We violated all that's ever sacred between people . . .

Odysseus reaches out and interlaces fingers with Athena . . .

INT. TEMPLE OF ATHENA, TROY – NIGHT (FLASHBACK)

Odysseus runs into the temple . . .

ODYSSEUS

(V.O.)

And turned a fight into a hunt.

Polites moves towards the STATUE OF ATHENA, sword DRAWN . . .

A GREEK SOLDIER THROWS a CRYING TROJAN WOMAN down in front of him . . .

SHE MAKES EYE CONTACT WITH ODYSSEUS – SHAKING HER HEAD, GREY EYES PLEADING FOR MERCY . . .

IT IS THE PERSON WE HAVE SEEN AS ATHENA –

Odysseus sees the Greek Soldier SWING HIS SWORD TOWARDS HER NECK AND WE MATCH-CUT TO:

Polites DECAPITATES the STATUE OF ATHENA, SPARKING, STONE HEAD TUMBLING onto the filthy marble floor of the temple . . .

ODYSSEUS
(V.O.)
To burn the walls of Troy was to burn the world entire . . .

Odysseus stands there, FROZEN, watching the stone head ROCK FROM SIDE TO SIDE as it comes to rest . . .

ODYSSEUS
(V.O.)
Including his home.

INT. MEGARON, PALACE OF ITHACA – NIGHT (BACK TO PRESENT)

Odysseus's hand is empty. 'Athena' is gone.

ODYSSEUS
What if he knew, that very night . . . ?

EXT. TROY – NIGHT (FLASHBACK)

Odysseus walks through the BURNING CITY, its VAST TOWERS COLLAPSING ALL AROUND HIM . . . BURNING, TUMBLING CHUNKS OF ARCHITECTURE LANDING IN FIERY CLOUDS, CRUSHING, DESTROYING . . . STATUES PULLED DOWN WITH ROPES . . . ARMAGEDDON . . .

ODYSSEUS
(V.O.)
As he walked through fires of anarchy and pain . . .

EXT. RUINS OF TROY – DAY (FLASHBACK)

Odysseus WATCHES thousands of Greek Warriors CELEBRATING in the ashes of Troy. Drunk. Appalling.

ODYSSEUS
(V.O.)
And in the days of sweaty celebrations to follow . . .

Someone KNOCKS Odysseus on the shoulder, but he does not react, STARING . . .

ODYSSEUS
(V.O.)
What if he knew exactly what he'd done?

INT. MEGARON, PALACE OF ITHACA – NIGHT (BACK TO PRESENT)

Penelope rests her head gently against the screen.

PENELOPE
What all of you had done.

Odysseus breathes . . .

ODYSSEUS
One man's idea. One man's trick to break Zeus's law forever.

He looks up at the stones and beams of the megaron, looming in the firelight . . .

ODYSSEUS
We lived in a world of palaces and trade and language . . . blind to its beauty until we broke it.

Penelope realizes something . . .

PENELOPE
<u>You</u> are the people from the sea . . .

ODYSSEUS

The breaking of Zeus's law is spreading like cancer. Our age of bronze is collapsing. And maybe he couldn't bear to see the ruins of what he'd done, anywhere. Least of all his home.

Odysseus rubs his face. Turns to the screen, glimpsing Penelope in the lamplight . . .

ODYSSEUS

But Odysseus is alive. And he'll be here when you need him most.

Penelope lifts her head, wipes a tear . . .

PENELOPE

Well, I've been living in his ruins long enough. Tomorrow I choose a husband.

Penelope RISES. SLIDES open the screen to address the megaron. Odysseus turns away, her beauty too bright . . . Telemachus and the servants looks up at Penelope, expectant . . .

PENELOPE

Bring the suitors at dawn.

Telemachus nods. Antinous and Polybus look at each other, nodding. Antinous puts his dagger away.

PENELOPE

Remove the arms from the hall.

Penelope gestures to the arms mounted all over the walls . . .

PENELOPE

In a few hours, one suitor will be happy and the rest angry, vengeful men. Bronze draws a man on, we'll have no weapons during the challenge and the doors will be locked. I'll marry whoever completes my trial.

Penelope disappears through the screen, shutting it behind her and continuing up to her bedchamber.

Telemachus watches Antinous and Polybus leave, then comes to Odysseus.

TELEMACHUS

How will we take on the Suitors?

ODYSSEUS

Not we. Their blood has to be on *my* hands. Or you'd face exile.

TELEMACHUS

Won't you?

ODYSSEUS

Just make sure they can't get those weapons.

Telemachus nods, hails Eumaeus.

TELEMACHUS

Gather servants you trust. Lock the arms in the upper storage room.

Eumaeus moves across the hall. Watched from the shadows by Melanthius . . .

TELEMACHUS

Even unarmed, there's so many of them. And you won't have a weapon.

ODYSSEUS

Oh, I'll have a weapon. Your mother's seen to that.

Telemachus looks at Odysseus, confused . . .

Servants pull BRONZE WEAPONS from the walls . . .

EXT. PALACE AT ITHACA – DAWN

A STORM lashes the palace as Suitors hurry towards it . . . THUNDER rumbles . . .

As the last Suitors enter, servants shut the GREAT DOORS, SLIDING A VAST BOLT ACROSS THE OUTSIDE.

INT. MEGARON, PALACE OF ITHACA – CONTINUOUS

Dozens of Suitors CROWD the megaron, watching as Servants lever flagstones up and drive AXES into the dirt beneath, forming a line of six pairs of axes TIED together leading to an upturned table.

A low RUMBLE of thunder . . . Peisander, a Suitor, leans in to Agelus, another Suitor . . .

PEISANDER

Zeus seems interested in the outcome.

Agelus looks at the axe heads in a line on the long table . . . the servants put an UPENDED TABLE at one end and a STOOL at the other . . .

AGELUS

But what's the trial?

Odysseus sits in a corner. Telemachus moves amongst the suitors, gauging their nervous energy. Antinous looks at the axe heads, wondering . . .

The heavy door behind the screen opens with a CLANG, and Melantho throws open the screen . . . the hubbub of the Suitors QUIETS as Penelope enters, in CEREMONIAL DRESS. POISED, BEAUTIFUL as she descends the steps CARRYING ODYSSEUS'S HUNTING BOW . . .

PENELOPE

For years, while my husband's been gone, you've commandeered this palace for your feasting. Your excuse was that you wanted to win my hand in marriage. As I've listened to you party and fight, corrupt my servants and disrespect my home, I've wanted nothing more than for Odysseus to return and see all this for himself.

She STOPS at the bottom step.

PENELOPE

But last night I realized that if he's not here now . . . he never will be. So I stand ready to marry anyone here who can string this hunting bow and shoot an arrow through those twelve axes. Step up and show me who you are . . .

She hands the great bow to Eumaeus. Who lovingly feels the weight of the bow . . .

EUMAEUS

Who's first?!

SILENCE. Penelope SMIRKS. Leodes, a Suitor, steps forward.

LEODES

Give me the bow.

Leodes takes the bow, unwinds its string, places one end of the bow on the stone floor and tries to bend the bow . . . he STRAINS and STRAINS.

PEISANDER

Alright, you've had your chance.

Leodes, breathless, gives the bow to Peisander, who tries to string it . . . and FAILS. He hands it back to Eumaeus, FRUSTRATED –

PEISANDER

It can't be done.

ANTINOUS

By you. As a boy I watched Odysseus do it with ease.

PEISANDER

Then you do it.

ANTINOUS

I'll wait my turn.

Polybus hails Melanthius –

POLYBUS

Light a fire, we'll warm the bow and oil it. This bow hasn't been strung in years.

INT. SAME – LATER

Polybus spins the bow in front of the fire, rubbing it with tallow.

Placing it against the floor, he puts his weight on the end, using all his strength to bend it . . . But can't.

The Suitors step up in turn, TRYING AND FAILING. Telemachus watches them, enjoying each failure . . . he takes the bow, walks over to Antinous, thrusting it at him . . .

TELEMACHUS

Your turn.

Antinous does not take the bow.

ANTINOUS

No need. My Queen's made her point.

He turns to Penelope, SINCERE . . .

ANTINOUS

We can't replace Odysseus. Some of us have always known that. Some of us would've followed that great man to Troy, if he'd let us. But he never came back, so choose the best of us here. Who've all failed your test.

ODYSSEUS

(O.S.)

I haven't.

The Suitors turn to notice Odysseus sitting to the side, head down.

ANTINOUS

Get this beggar out of here.

EUMAEUS

The doors are locked until the trial's over.

ANTINOUS

The trial's over.

ODYSSEUS

I want to try.

The Suitors LAUGH . . .

LEODES

Give it a rest, old man.

ANTINOUS

I told you to get him out of here.

EUMAEUS

He has the right to try.

Odysseus gets up, shuffles over to Telemachus, who looks at Antinous.

TELEMACHUS

If you won't, he may as well.

Antinous looks at Telemachus with utter contempt.

ANTINOUS

You're making a mockery of your mother's wishes.

Telemachus hands the bow to Odysseus, and leans in to Antinous . . .

TELEMACHUS

(whispers)

My mother's wishes are for you all to burn.

Odysseus takes the bow, sits on the stool at the end of the long table. He TURNS it in his hands, feeling its weight.

ELATUS

He's an old archer!

LAUGHTER . . . Odysseus puts his ear to the bow, TAPPING the wood experimentally . . .

AGELUS

Oooh, an expert!

ELATUS

Show us how it's done, plate licker!

More laughter. Odysseus puts one end on the floor, pulls the string taught and puts pressure on the bow, WHICH DOES NOT BEND . . . Telemachus FROWNS, looks over to see his mother turn and start up the stairs . . .

Odysseus rubs his palm, blows on it, takes up the string, once again pushing down on the end. WITHOUT BENDING IT.

The Suitors JEER.

LEODES

Forget it.

Telemachus now looks WORRIED. Penelope passes through the screen towards the HEAVY DOORS . . .

Eumaeus steps forward to take the bow . . .

EUMAEUS

Okay, friend. That's enough.

But Odysseus FLIPS the bow, once, twice, sticks the end on the floor – BENDS IT, STRINGS IT –

The JEERING CEASES.

Odysseus PLUCKS the bow – A MIGHTY 'TWANG!' ECHOES THROUGH THE HALL . . .

Penelope PAUSES, head half-turned . . .

Eumaeus TURNS to the sound, AMAZED . . .

Antinous BOLTS, AS HE DID AS A CHILD, RUNNING for the door . . .

Odysseus mounts an arrow to the string –

Odysseus aims the bow, horizontal, and FIRES THE ARROW THROUGH ALL TWELVE AXE HEADS – THUMP! VIBRATING IN THE UPTURNED TABLE . . .

Polybus, marvelling at the feat, looks at Antinous running away, confused –

Odysseus loads his bow . . .

POLYBUS

Antinous – ?

Polybus turns to Odysseus, REALIZING –

POLYBUS

You're Odysseus – !

Odysseus FIRES at Polybus, hitting him in the THROAT . . . Suitors SCRAMBLE AWAY . . .

VARIOUS

Odysseus! Odysseus! He's back!

Eumaeus GRABS Telemachus's sleeve –

EUMAEUS

Is it him?!

TELEMACHUS

Yes. Secure the weapons.

Penelope steps through the heavy doors, Melantho tries to follow.

PENELOPE

Surely your place is down there.

THE HEAVY DOORS SLAM SHUT BEHIND PENELOPE, leaving Melantho in the hall, TERRIFIED . . .

Polybus DROPS. The Suitors look at Odysseus loading another arrow – PANICKING, DIVING for cover – Odysseus PICKS OFF TWO, THREE, FOUR more as they run . . .

Antinous, at the far end of the hall, GRABS Melanthius –

ANTINOUS

Where are the weapons?!

MELANTHIUS

The upper storeroom.

ANTINOUS

GO!

Behind Odysseus, Suitors GRAB the upturned table and RACE towards him, TABLE AS SHIELD –

TELEMACHUS

DAD!

Odysseus SPINS, the table SMASHES INTO HIM . . .

INT. UPPER CORRIDOR – CONTINUOUS

Melanthius RACES down the corridor, SPURS JANGLING. He THROWS the storage room door open and BOLTS inside . . .

INT. UPPER STORAGE ROOM – CONTINUOUS

Melanthius takes in the piles of bronze, GRABS at spears –

EUMAEUS
(O.S.)

I told you – too loud, cowherd.

Melanthius SPINS to see Eumaeus SLAM the door on him.

INT. UPPER CORRIDOR – CONTINUOUS

Eumaeus LOCKS the door.

INT. MEGARON, PALACE OF ITHACA – CONTINUOUS

Odysseus GOES DOWN, the table on top of him, then PUSHES off the floor, FLIPPING the table over him, Suitors FLAILING – Odysseus loads his bow, FIRES – hitting a Suitor –

Telemachus sees an AXE SMASH through the ceiling, BLOW after BLOW . . .

INT. UPPER STORAGE ROOM – CONTINUOUS

Melanthius uses a BRONZE AXE to HACK a hole in the floor –

INT. MEGARON, PALACE OF ITHACA – CONTINUOUS

Odysseus DRAWS an arrow from his quiver – Leodes PUNCHES – RUSHES Odysseus – Odysseus HEADBUTTS him – Leodes goes down, PULLING the quiver off Odysseus's shoulder – Odysseus STABS him with the arrow as Elatus TACKLES him – they TUMBLE – Odysseus's rags are ripped off him, he has LEATHER ARMOUR underneath –

INT. UPPER STORAGE ROOM – CONTINUOUS

Melanthius DROPS the axe through the hole he's made . . .

INT. MEGARON, PALACE OF ITHACA – CONTINUOUS

Telemachus sees the BRONZE AXE DROP. A Suitor GRABS the axe, feels its heft. A SPEAR DROPS next . . . Telemachus TURNS and RUNS towards the upper corridor . . .

Odysseus LIFTS Elatus, pushes him towards the long table – BURIES his face on the back of one of the twelve axes – TURNS – a Suitor BEARS down with a BRONZE AXE – Odysseus ROLLS away as the axe SMASHES into the table – Odysseus GRABS the handle as the bronze axe lodges in the long table, but the Suitor YANKS it up again – Odysseus ROLLS as the axe SWINGS – STRIKING the nearest axe head, SPARKING, DISLODGING it from the dirt –

At the back of the crowd Antinous AGITATES –

ANTINOUS

What're you waiting for?! He's going to kill us all!

Odysseus GRABS the pair of axes tied together, as the Suitor RAISES his bronze axe, Odysseus SWINGS tied axes into the Suitor's face –

INT. UPPER CORRIDOR – CONTINUOUS

Telemachus RACES down the corridor – UNLOCKS the door –

INT. MEGARON, PALACE OF ITHACA – CONTINUOUS

Odysseus SWINGS WILDLY with the TIED AXES at the nearest Suitors, clearing a space around his fallen bow . . . a SPEAR flies past his nose, STICKING into the column behind him – he DUCKS, SPINS around the column as MORE SPEARS come –

INT. UPPER STORAGE ROOM – CONTINUOUS

Telemachus CHARGES at Melanthius, who is dropping SWORDS through the hole – Melanthius spots him, raises a sword in defence . . . Telemachus GRABS a sword from the pile . . .

INT. MEGARON, PALACE OF ITHACA – CONTINUOUS

Odysseus DUCKS spears as he SWINGS THE AXES, taking out Suitors . . . a SWORD hacks into his arm – he looks up – Antinous has a SWORD – a suitor STANDS on the axe head – PUSHES Odysseus from his axe, Odysseus stumbles back, tripping over bodies . . .

INT. UPPER STORAGE ROOM – CONTINUOUS

Telemachus and Melanthius exchange blows . . .

INT. MEGARON, PALACE OF ITHACA – CONTINUOUS

Odysseus, UNARMED, steps back over the bodies, Antinous and the last six fighting Suitors threatening with SPEARS and SWORDS, Odysseus desperately looks for a weapon, YANKS an arrow from a dead suitor, holds it up like a dagger. Antinous LAUGHS . . .

ANTINOUS

Did you think you could kill all of us?

ODYSSEUS

Long as I kill you.

They move closer and closer, PRODDING him with spears, DRAWING BLOOD . . . like the end of a BEAR HUNT . . . Odysseus looks around, DESPERATE –

TELEMACHUS

(O.S.)

DAD!

Odysseus looks up – Telemachus DROPS a BRONZE SWORD to Odysseus – he CATCHES it, CHOPS spears in half – charges Antinous – who tries to exchange blows with him, but is forced back, even as BROKEN SPEARS are THRUST at Odysseus's side and back –

Antinous goes down – the SAVAGE ODYSSEUS on top of him, broken spears sticking out of him LIKE A BULL AT ITS END IN THE RING . . . Odysseus has his sword at Antinous's throat –

ODYSSEUS

(breathless rasp)

When you see Sinon in Hades . . . Tell him I'll head west to honour my men . . .

He pulls out the wooden lot and, with bloody fingers, stuffs it into Antinous's mouth . . .

ODYSSEUS

And that I gave you back your shame.

He RUNS the sword through Antinous. ROLLS off him, spears dislodging. Stands, pulling the remaining rags from his back, BLOODY in his leather armour. He surveys the CARNAGE in the hall . . . the remaining Suitors are ON THEIR KNEES . . .

The THUNDER of Zeus ROLLS around the megaron . . .

Odysseus DROPS his bronze sword with a CLATTER . . . STUMBLES BREATHLESSLY through the hall, stepping over DEAD SUITORS . . .

Telemachus comes into the hall. Sees his father walk. Starts BANGING his sword against the ground in time with Odysseus's steps . . .

ODYSSEUS
(V.O.)
We broke the fragile bonds between men . . .

BANG! BANG! BANG! The surviving suitors and servants SMACK the ground, taking up the rhythm of Odysseus's PAINFUL WALK . . .

BANG! *INSERT CUT: Greek Soldiers* BEATING TIME *with their* SPEARS *against wood as they* LINE THE DOCK AT ITHACA . . .

As walks he looks at his son . . . nods . . . forces himself up the stairs, his BLOODY HANDS FUMBLE in his belt . . .

ODYSSEUS
(V.O.)
And for centuries of darkness to follow, the stories of Troy will only be sung . . .

BANG! *INSERT CUT: Telemachus,* DRESSED AS A KING, *leads Penelope down the dock as the Soldiers* BEAT TIME . . .

The heavy doors OPEN . . . Penelope is there . . . Odysseus STUMBLES towards her . . .

Eumaeus BEATS his stick against the floor . . .

BANG! *INSERT CUT: Telemachus, as king, leads Penelope to a* SHIP, *approaching a* FIGURE *from behind who is checking the rigging. She turns to Telemachus,* TEARS STREAMING, *embraces her son . . .*

BANG!

Odysseus STEPS towards Penelope, raising a BLOODY HAND HOLDING A GOLDEN PIN . . .

The banging STOPS. Silence.

Penelope takes the pin and looks down to see the GOLD ATHENA ENCIRCLED BY VINES . . . she looks up at Odysseus, MELTING . . .

He COLLAPSES, slumped at the top of the steps . . .

Penelope takes him in her arms, wiping blood from his eyes . . .

PENELOPE
Odysseus. My love, you came back.

ODYSSEUS
At last. At the end . . . to see my beloved Ithaca one last time . . .

Penelope RUNS her hands across him, desperate . . .

PENELOPE
No, no, no . . . you can't, not now, I've waited so long . . .

She holds his face, looks into his face, tears streaming . . .

PENELOPE
You can't die . . .

ODYSSEUS
Not death. *Exile* . . .

And he SMILES at her . . .

BANG! *INSERT CUT: as Penelope boards the ship, the Figure turns from the rigging –* IT IS ODYSSEUS, *bandaged, beard trimmed. Telemachus is on the dock, waving . . .*

Penelope looks down at bloody Odysseus . . .

ODYSSEUS
Telemachus will be king. And we'll head into the unknown west to honour my men. Together . . .

BANG! *INSERT CUT: pushing* LOW *through* WAVES *at sunset . . .*

She smiles at him . . .

PENELOPE

Take your fastest ship and brightest crew and head for the horizon . . . ?

Odysseus nods.

ODYSSEUS

Chasing the escaping sun . . .

EXT. SHIP – EVENING

As the ship rows west, Penelope and Odysseus stand at the front, looking to the warming horizon . . .

PENELOPE

Why will the stories only be sung?

ODYSSEUS

Because songs will be all they have to remember those of us who could write.

Penelope looks at Odysseus . . . takes his hands in hers . . .

PENELOPE

Civilization will rise again . . .

Odysseus thinks . . . nods . . .

EXT. TROY – NIGHT

Odysseus STUMBLES in the FLAMING RUINS of Troy, breathing hard, on one knee, sweaty in the firelight, he looks up, APPALLED.

ODYSSEUS

(V.O.)

A new dawn will break over the darkened world . . .

The Vast Wooden Horse, AFLAME, listing sickly, FALLS SIDEWAYS, SMOKE AND FLAME TRAILING . . .

ODYSSEUS
(V.O.)
And our mistakes will once again be forgotten.

The Horse JAMS *against the Temple of Athena.* BURNING. BURNING. *And we –*

FADE OUT.

CREDITS.

END.